UNIX Fundamentals: UNIX Basics

...

by Kevin Reichard

MIS:
PRESS

A Subsidiary of
Henry Holt and Co., Inc.

First Edition—1994

Printed in the United States of America.

Library of Congress Cataloging-in-Publication Data

Reichard, Kevin.
  UNIX fundamentals. UNIX basics/Kevin Reichard.
        p.   cm.
    Includes index.
    ISBN 1-55828-362-5 : $19.95
    1. UNIX (Computer file) 2. Operating systems (Computers)
  I. Title.
  QA76.76.063R444   1994
  005.4'3--dc20   94-30873
                                                             CIP

10 9 8 7 6 5 4 3 2 1

MIS:Press books are available at special discounts for bulk purchases for sales promotions, premiums, fund-raising, or educational use. Special editions or book excerpts can also be created to specification.

For details contact: Special Sales Director
                            MIS:Press
                            a subsidiary of Henry Holt and Company, Inc.
                            115 West 18th Street
                            New York, New York 10011

Publisher: Brenda McLaughlin   Assoc. Production Editor: Erika Putre
Development Editor: Laura Lewin   Technical Editor: Eric Johnson
Production Editor: Anne Alessi   Copy Editor: Suzanne Ingrao

▪ TABLE OF CONTENTS ▪

▼

CHAPTER FOUR ▪ LEARNING ABOUT YOUR ENVIRONMENT AND THE SHELL 125

CHAPTER FIVE ▪ COMMUNICATION, NETWORKING AND ELECTRONIC MAIL 157

CHAPTER SIX ▪ TEXT EDITING, PROCESSING, AND PRINTING   187

▼

▼

▪ INTRODUCTION ▪

Welcome to *UNIX Fundamentals: The Basics!* If you're a beginning UNIX user, or an experienced computer user working with UNIX for the first time, you'll find that this book occupies a unique niche in the UNIX computer-publishing field: It is the *only* text written solely for end users. It's not written for UNIX system administrators or UNIX gurus. And it's not written for anyone having a ton of experience having computing—never mind the UNIX operating system.

Who Should Read This Book?

UNIX Fundamentals is geared for the true UNIX neophyte. Even so, it still needs to be geared to a very wide group of people. A UNIX neophyte could be someone who's never worked with any sort of computer and was distressed and amazed to find that UNIX usage was a central part of a new job or a promotion. A UNIX neophyte could also be someone who has worked on a PC clone or a Macintosh, but who has not been exposed to the more powerful world of UNIX computing.

These two extremes cover an awful lot of ground, particularly considering how many people actually use UNIX—upwards of 80 million people, according to some estimates from market-research firms. Still,

▼

even when dealing with such a large potential audience, there are some commonalities among those who should be reading this book. By and large, this book was written for the vast majority of UNIX end users, who typically:

▲ Work on larger, networked, multiuser systems.

▲ Have access to a system administrator.

▲ Work mostly with one or two applications.

▲ Do not consider themselves UNIX gurus or experienced computer users.

This last point is key. This book is not written as a primer on every single aspect of the UNIX operating system. If you're looking for a more complete UNIX tutorial or a comprehensive reference work, there are further listings of recommended works in the Appendix.

Past these generalities, however, there's not necessarily a lot to unite the vast number of UNIX end users. There's a version of UNIX for virtually every kind of computer—everything from a personal computer to a Cray supercomputer. In that fashion, the advice presented here doesn't make any assumptions about hardware configurations.

If you're using a personal computer running SCO UNIX, you'll find that this book is applicable to your needs. If you're using a Sun Microsystems workstation in an academic environment, you'll find that this book is applicable to your needs. If you're using a VT102 terminal hooked up to a more powerful computer, you'll find that this book is applicable to your needs. And if you're using an X terminal linked to a larger network, you'll find that this book is applicable to your needs.

Obviously, a book like this cannot be written to the specific needs of every end user. For instance, there's not a lot of discussion of information *specific* to UNIX workstations, nor information *specific* to personal computers or Cray supercomputers. Virtually every type of computer has been configured at one time or another to run the UNIX operating system—you can even buy a version of UNIX for the Commodore

▼

Amiga!—and so focusing on a specific type of computer, such as a workstation, would be too limiting when considering the goals of this book.

Assumptions About You, the User

As stated above, the assumption is that you, dear reader, have never used the UNIX operating system and are unfamiliar with its practices. The assumption also is that you're not very familiar with computing in general. Because of these assumptions, you'll find that Chapter 1, "Getting Started with UNIX", starts at ground zero when it comes to computing in general and UNIX specifically.

Examples in This Book

There are many examples used within to illuminate concepts and practices. With every UNIX system being different, there's the real danger that the examples cannot be used by every UNIX end user.

Always remember, however, that even if the specific example isn't applicable to your specific situation, the general concepts behind the example are applicable to the vast majority of UNIX systems.

For instance, something as mundane as logging in a UNIX system varies from system to system. However, virtually every UNIX system requires a login procedure of one form or another. In this instance, what's important is not the actual set of keystrokes that logs you in a system, but the procedure of logging in a system and the concepts behind the need for logins.

▼

Reality Checks

Throughout this book, UNIX usage will be treated in two ways: The ways things should work in theory, and the way things sometimes work in the real world—or not work, as the case may be. For instance, the opening chapter of this book deals with the nasty fact that things can go wrong with something as mundane as logging on a system, and what you should when something does go wrong. The way things usually work is detailed in special sections entitled "Reality Checks", which will detail how you should deal with the times when UNIX doesn't quite work the way it should.

Command Reference Tables

When a new UNIX command is introduced, you'll also find a Command Reference within the same section. These references exist for two reasons: They summarize the main points from the text, and they also are designed to stand out when you inevitably return to the text to review information about a command or procedure. The Command Reference will use the same layout throughout the book:

- ▲ **Command syntax.** This details exactly how you use the command.
- ▲ **Purpose.** One or two sentences summarize what the command does.
- ▲ **Options.** Virtually every command features options, which change the way the command works.

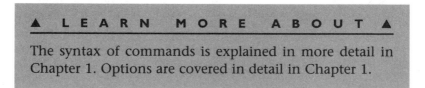

▲ L E A R N   M O R E   A B O U T ▲

The syntax of commands is explained in more detail in Chapter 1. Options are covered in detail in Chapter 1.

▼

Conventions Used in This Book

We've created a very *user-friendly* (agreed, it's a trite phrase, but so appropriate here) book to help you wade through the very confusing world of UNIX computing. Some of these features include:

▲ Commands that are to be typed directly into the UNIX system are indicated by the `monospaced` font.

▲ Keystrokes—that is, keys you press as part of your UNIX system usage, such as **Enter** key—are indicated by the **bold** type.

▲ Filenames and directories are also in **bold** type.

▲ Machine names and electronic-mail addresses are marked by the *italic* type.

This Book's Structure

If you take a peek at the contents and then look at the page numbers, you'll find that close to half of this book is filled by Chapters 1, 2, and 3. This is no mistake, but the result of some careful planning. The first three chapters cover UNIX, as well as computing in general, on a very basic level. These chapters form the basis of your computing knowledge, and as such computing concepts are presented in very detailed fashion, supported by a slew of examples.

This book is the inaugural effort in an ambitious series of books, UNIX Fundamentals, dedicated toward UNIX end users. As such, this book serves as a roadmap for the rest of the series—Chapters 4–10 are more general and introductory than Chapters 1–3. For instance, Chapter 5, "Communications, Networking, and Electronic Mail," is merely an introduction to a very wide-open topic—and a topic that warrants its own book, so you can look for a communications book down the road as part of this series.

Acknowledgments

Many people were central in bringing this book to your hands:

▲ Laura Lewin, a very patient editor

▲ Nelson King, a frequent coffee companion and sounding board

▲ Steve Berkowitz, the publisher at MIS:Press

▲ The members of the CompuServe UNIX Forum (particularly George L. Smythe and Caroll Ford), who provide a very useful window in the world of UNIX users

Feedback

I'd love to hear your comments about this book—good, bad, or ugly. If you're connected in some way to the Internet you can send me electronic mail at kreichard@mcimail.com (don't worry if you have no idea about what this means—we'll cover the Internet and electronic mail in Chapter 5). If you have a CompuServe account, you can drop me a note there (my account number is 73670,3422). Or, if your UNIX system is not connected to the Internet, you can drop me a line in care of MIS:Press, 115 W. 18th St., New York, NY 10011.

▪ CHAPTER ONE ▪
Getting Started with UNIX

The operating system controls every portion of the computer system. This chapter introduces UNIX, a typical UNIX computer system, and some elementary procedures you'll use every day. Topics include:

- ▲ What makes UNIX so unique.
- ▲ What you'll need to know about UNIX as you do your daily work.
- ▲ The different types of UNIX installations.
- ▲ Why a system administrator is important.
- ▲ Using terminals on the network.
- ▲ Using the UNIX prompt.
- ▲ Special keys used by UNIX.
- ▲ Sorting through the different versions of UNIX.
- ▲ Using a text-based interface.
- ▲ Using a graphical interface.
- ▲ How to deal with UNIX commands.
- ▲ How to login and logoff a UNIX system.

▼

What is UNIX?

Before you get started, let's take a moment and discuss exactly what UNIX is and how you'll use it.

UNIX is an *operating system*. That is, it's the software that actually controls the computer hardware. If you've used a computer, you've probably had some contact with an operating system, either directly (with MS-DOS) or indirectly (the Macintosh or *Windows* hides many of the messy details by interacting directly with the operating system instead of leaving it to you).

Without an operating system, a click on the keyboard or a swipe with a mouse would be little more than physical actions unintelligible to the computer. There is nothing particularly magic about this process: For instance, when you press the **A** key, the keyboard sends a signal to the computer, which in turn notifies the operating system that a key was pressed. The operating system then interprets your action as a letter *A* and sends that information to the appropriate locations, whether it be another program or another section of the operating system. In short, it's the operating system that interprets this physical action. When you print a letter, it's actually the operating system telling the computer where to send the letter and in what form. And if there are many users on your computer system, the operating system acts as a traffic cop, making sure all needs are met in a reasonable period of time.

This may sound a little daunting, but don't worry. If you're like the average computer user, you're not going to spend a lot of time dealing with the operating system— on the order of 7 percent of your computing time, according to various studies. By and large, you won't need to worry whether the system is properly talking to the printer, or whether your computer is properly talking to the rest of the network. There are people to handle those kinds of details—they are called *system administrators*, and their job is to make sure your computer system works properly. They'll be the ones working with the guts of the computer system.

In fact, your main use of UNIX will be somewhat indirect, as you arrive at UNIX's main reason for existence as far as you're concerned: its ability to run **applications**. Whether it be a database-management system like *Oracle or Informix*, a computer-aided-design package like *AutoCAD*, a desktop-publishing system like *FrameMaker*, or a custom application designed for your company, you'll spend most of your time actually using the application and not UNIX.

So why bother learning UNIX?

Because, for certain tasks, interaction with the operating system is inevitable when it comes to routine daily chores, like copying files, editing text, and electronic mail. In these cases, a good working knowledge of some UNIX commands will make your life much simpler. Also, a working knowledge of how the operating system works will assist you when working with applications. For instance, knowing how UNIX stores files and organizes directories is necessary knowledge no matter what the application.

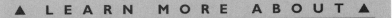

▲ L E A R N   M O R E   A B O U T ▲

In this chapter, you'll begin with an overview of some UNIX conventions and concepts, then you'll move to an explanation of how you'll give commands directly to UNIX.

UNIX and Your Computer System

If you're like most UNIX users, you're working on a larger computer system that supports many other users, either within your department or throughout your company. This is the sort of situation where UNIX shines, thanks to some very distinctive characteristics of the UNIX operating system:

▲ **UNIX is a multiuser operating system.** This means that more than one person can be using the operating system— and therefore the computer system—at one time. It also means that many users can use the same files if need be.

▲ **UNIX is a multitasking operating system.** UNIX has the ability to do more than one thing at once—obviously an important trait when there are many people using the

▼

computer system at once. This also allows *you* to perform more than one chore on the computer system at one time (which we'll cover in Chapter 9).

▲ **With UNIX, networking is built into the operating system.** You probably aren't working directly on the main computer running UNIX. Instead, you're probably working on a terminal connected to the main computer. The network connects you, but you don't need to worry about actually using this network—it's all automatic with UNIX.

A Typical UNIX Installation

As you'll learn quickly, there is no such thing as a "typical" UNIX computer system. UNIX was designed from the beginning to run on virtually every type of computer hardware, and so we have a situation right now where UNIX is installed on everything ranging from a personal computer to a Cray supercomputer.

There are some common types of UNIX installations, however, and it is likely that one of these configurations comes fairly close to how you work.

▲ A large number of users are connected directly to a *server*. A server is a large computer that controls everything that happens on the network—it distributes information to all users, keeps track of the data used by all users, and coordinates communications between users. In this case, the server is running the UNIX operating system, although not every network uses UNIX. And because all of the information is stored on one machine, it is said to have a single *filesystem*, as shown in Figure 1.1.

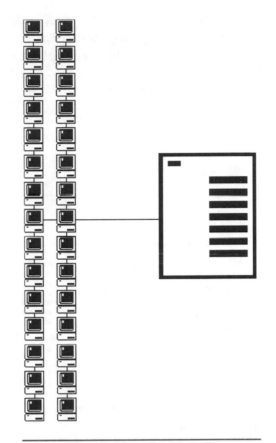

FIGURE 1.1 A large UNIX-based network

▲   Two sets of users are connected to servers, which in turn
    communicate with each other. The servers fulfill the same
    roles as those described in the previous example, with one
    major difference: They also manage communications
    between the two servers, which don't necessarily need to be
    located in the same office (or city or state, for that matter).
    However, you don't need to worry about how these servers
    communicate, or that communications are occurring—

UNIX and your system administrator take care of those details. For instance, although there are two different servers with their own information storage, to you it will look like there is only one filesystem. As far as you're concerned, it's just one big network, as shown in Figure 1.2.

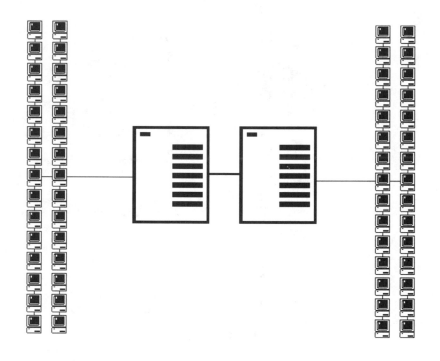

FIGURE 1.2 Two servers and a large network

▲ Five computers running UNIX are connected on a network. These computers optimized for running UNIX are called *workstations*. There's not one main server in this illustration; UNIX can run without a main server when the local computers have enough computing horsepower to run UNIX on their own, which is the case with these workstations, as shown in Figure 1.3.

FIGURE 1.3 Five workstations on their own network

A UNIX network is a flexible creature. A network can be installed to serve the needs of a single department, an entire company site, or several company sites. Several sites? Yes. With the aid of telecommunications equipment, a UNIX network can be set up in several different sites, although to the end user the network may appear as one physical entity. Your company may have a setup where the disk drives located in the home office in Sioux City, Iowa, look like they're part of your local UNIX system. (In this case, you'd have two filesystems that are connected to look as one.) As a user, usually you don't need to worry about this.

However, you don't need to be on a network to use the UNIX operating system. Though most UNIX users are indeed networked in a corporate or university setting, it's certainly not a prerequisite. For instance, many home computer users are running a version of UNIX—usually Linux, BSD386, or Coherent—on their home computers. Similarly, many professionals and scientists need the power of a specialized program and buy a UNIX workstation for that specific purpose.

Your Link to the Network

In the UNIX world, the equipment used directly by you, the user, is called a *terminal*. A terminal is usually made up of a monitor and a keyboard, and perhaps a mouse if you're working on a graphical system.

A terminal may come in several different forms: A UNIX ASCII terminal (which displays characters but not graphics), a PC or Macintosh running its own software but still connected to a network, a PC or Macintosh running UNIX, a UNIX workstation, or an X terminal optimized for graphics.

▼

You won't need to know specifically what sort of terminal you're using at this point in your UNIX education, but you do need to know how your terminal fits into the typical UNIX network. Figure 1.4 shows a rough approximation of such a setup, although—and this is true of the UNIX world as a whole, which you'll learn time and time again—your specific situation may differ.

FIGURE 1.4 A typical UNIX terminal setup

In and of itself, the terminal won't allow you to do a whole lot, unless you happen to be using a PC or Macintosh running its own operating system. (In this case, however, you won't be very useful to your company if you aren't connected to the network.) The key to the terminal is its connection to the UNIX network. As you can see from Figure 1.5, the three terminals are linked to a server. The server controls what is displayed on the terminals.

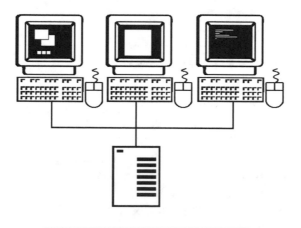

FIGURE 1.5 A small UNIX network

▼

As far as UNIX networks go, the network shown in Figure 1.5 is on the smaller side—but there's no such thing as a "typical" UNIX network. In this case, UNIX controls all the communications between the three terminals and the server.

As you can tell, the server occupies a very important role in the UNIX network. However, you won't have to worry too much about the server. Most companies employ a specific worker, the *system administrator*, to make sure the server runs smoothly and efficiently. The system administrator is also charged with many of the day-to-day chores that should make your computing experiences go smoothly.

There is one part of the server that you'll need to know about: The disk storage. Your terminal relies on the storage capabilities of the server when it comes to saving your work. These storage capabilities come in the form of floppy disks, hard disk (also called hard drives or fixed disks), tape drives, and CD-ROM drives. You won't need to know exactly what storage method is used in your UNIX system, however.

Using the Terminal

No matter what, your UNIX usage will occur on at least two computer elements: A *keyboard* and a *monitor*. The monitor may be small or large, color or monochrome; your only concern is to make sure it's turned on.

This consideration must not be ignored; you'd be surprised at the number of beginning computer users who freak out when they get no response from the computer, only to discover that the monitor was not turned on. The lesson here is not to be embarrassed by obvious mistakes, but rather learn from them.

Take a look at your monitor when UNIX is running. Somewhere on the screen, you'll see a blinking line. This is called the *cursor*. When

▼

you press a key on the keyboard, the character on the key will appear where the cursor was.

As for the keyboard—well, sad to say, there's no such thing as a standard keyboard in the UNIX world, though there's a growing reliance on personal-computer-type keyboards in new systems from the likes of Hewlett-Packard. But we can't take for granted that everyone will be using a PC-style keyboard, so this book won't make any assumptions about keys specific to vendors. Not every keyboard features a **Help** key, for instance, so there never will be advice about hitting the **Help** key when you run into a problem (though, if your keyboard features a **Help** key, it can't hurt to use it).

There are a few keys that you should locate and commit to memory, however:

▲ The **Return** key is used extensively in any computing experience. The **Return** key is used to send commands to the system, for instance. The **Return** key goes under a few different labels, however, including **Enter** and ↵. Some keyboards feature a **Return** key on the right side of the keyboard, while other keyboard place an additional **Return** key on the bottom-right of the keyboard, next to the numeric keypad.

▲ The **Backspace** key, sometimes labeled as **BackSpace**, **BkSp**, or ←, is used to delete the character immediately preceding the cursor. Sometimes, however, the key you want to delete remains on the screen, even though the cursor has moved. This is normal; the character is indeed erased, and anything new you type in will appear in the place of the erased character.

Be warned that this isn't 100 percent true in the UNIX world; sometimes the **Backspace** key deletes the character *following* the cursor, and sometimes the **Backspace** key doesn't do anything at all.

▼

▲ The **Delete** (or **Del**) key is used to delete or erase characters following the cursor. (On some older keyboards, the **Delete** key is labeled **RUBOUT**.) That's the theory, anyway; don't count on it being true 100 percent of the time. Sometimes the **Delete** key is used to quit in the middle of running a command. If your **Delete** key doesn't delete characters, tell your system administrator; there are some simple steps they can take to make sure that your **Delete** character works.

▲ The **Control** (or **Ctrl**) character may appear in many locations on a keyboard—sometimes above the **Shift** key, sometimes below, sometimes to the right of the **Space bar**, sometimes to the left, sometimes in both locations—but it's worthwhile to commit its location to memory, since the **Ctrl** key is one of the important keys you'll encounter in your day-to-day UNIX usage. Why is it so important? Because it's used to extend the functionality of the keyboard in some very specific ways. Think of the **Ctrl** key as a pumped-up **Shift** key, adding one more use to the current set of keys. Throughout this book, there will be many references to **Ctrl**-key combinations. When typing them, first press down the **Ctrl** key, followed by the second key, much in the same fashion you'd use the **Shift** key.

This is technical

In documentation, the **Ctrl** character is sometimes shown as a **^**; in this instance, **Ctrl-U** and **^U** do the same thing. However, this is a rather confusing practice, since virtually every keyboard also features a key with a caret, or **^**; if you run into documentation that uses the caret, do *not* type the caret key on the keyboard. Because of the possibility for confusion, this book will not use **^** as a substitute for the **Ctrl** key.

You'd be surprised at the number of circumstances **Ctrl**-key combinations become extremely handy. For instance, many early UNIX keyboards lacked a **Delete** key, so the **Ctrl** key was used in conjunction with

▼

another key to provide this function: **Ctrl-H**. UNIX still supports **Ctrl-H** as a substitute for the **Delete** key. Other handy **Ctrl**-key combinations include **Ctrl-D** (which interrupts whatever action the UNIX system is performing), **Ctrl-S** (which pauses output to the monitor), **Ctrl-Q** (which starts the paused output), and **Ctrl-U** (which erases an entire line).

Some Quick Words of Advice

As you get going, there are a few things you should *always* remember when you're using UNIX.

▲ **There's very little damage you can do to a UNIX system.** Most computer systems are set up to minimize the amount of chaos you can create by incorrect commands or actions. That's especially true of UNIX systems, where important information is protected from beginning or casual users. While there are times you should take a few safeguards in your computing chores—and these steps will be explained further in this book—you shouldn't be fearful about experimentation.

▲ **Nothing in this book is an absolute.** UNIX comes in many different flavors and versions. Some of the commands covered in this book may not be available with your particular UNIX system.

Don't worry if you try something detailed in this book and discover than it doesn't work on your system. Chances are that you're doing everything correctly; the shortcoming lies with your system.

▲ **Every system is different.** The procedures describes within this book are going to be true for the majority of UNIX users. However, a strength of UNIX is the fact that it can be changed and adapted easily, and each UNIX installation is slightly different.

▼

Don't be surprised if some of the procedures described here don't apply to your system, or if something you consider crucial to your system isn't covered here.

▲ **Befriend your system administrator.** The system administrator is the person charged with making sure your UNIX system runs smoothly and efficiently. Don't be afraid to ask questions or request short demonstrations. And don't forget: Most UNIX system administrators can be bribed with M&Ms.

UNIX Versions: There are many different implementations of UNIX. This stems directly from UNIX's roots as an operating system developed by Bell Labs, the AT&T research lab, which (prebreakup) was prohibited by regulators from selling computer-related products. As a result of this regulation, AT&T could only give away UNIX for research purposes. However, companies and universities were not subject to the same limitations, so they were free to resell it.

To make a long story short, many slightly different versions of UNIX made their way to the market, as every vendor added their own perception of value. Thus, you have brand names like UNIX, XENIX, SunOS, Solaris, HP-UX, AIX, UnixWare, SCO UNIX, Ultrix, A/UX, Linux, Mach, OSF/1, and Coherent available from various and sundry vendors. These products by and large support UNIX commands and run programs written for UNIX, whether or not they are technically UNIX (which would involve a rather long, involved, and boring explanation, so we'll skip it). Remember that the brand name differs from vendor to vendor, but at the core is the UNIX operating system.

Commands

Accomplishing anything with UNIX relies on two steps: Determining what you want to do, and then telling the computer in a manner it can understand.

The first step is the more difficult of the two. To tell the computer what you want done, you need to frame it in terms the computer can understand. Typing something like, "Print out my report," won't accomplish very much on *any* computer system, much less a UNIX system.

Instead, you'll need to determine the proper UNIX command needed to accomplish your task. A *command* is exactly what the name says: A direct instruction to the UNIX system. There are literally hundreds of UNIX commands, but you don't need to know them all. Generally speaking, you'll be able to get by with working knowledge of a dozen or so commands in the beginning and gradually working your way into the UNIX command set as needed. You can either consult with your system administrator about specific commands, or you can purchase one of many guides to UNIX commands (a few recommended guides are listed in the Appendix).

In fact, it's important up front to know exactly *how* commands work. After an explanation of the concepts behind commands, it will be easier to explain exactly how to enter commands in your system.

Commands Are Your Friends—Really

As stated earlier, a command is nothing more than a direct instruction to the UNIX system. Commands can be mundane, such as listing the contents of the computer, or they can be more elaborate. Typically, commands are rather cryptic and not very logical to the average end user.

Take, for example, the command that lists the information stored on the computer: **ls**. Now, this isn't exactly the most intuitive of commands, and knowing that **ls** is short-hand for *list* doesn't raise the intuition level. It's one of those things where you memorize a command because you'll end up using it so much.

Entering a command is very simple: Type the command at the command prompt and then press the **Return** key. Simple? Well, not for a true beginner—there's a lot of turf to cover before you get to that point.

And, quite honestly, there *is* more to entering a command than just typing it in. Most UNIX commands do very little in and of themselves, unless you're entering some next-to-worthless command like **date** to see what date the system thinks today is. Most commands require *arguments*, which essentially contain additional information that more specifically describes what you want the command to accomplish. Generally speaking, arguments fall into two categories: *options* and *filenames*. Options are command-specific, while a filename can be any file on the UNIX system you have access to.

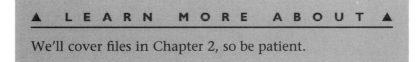

▲ L E A R N   M O R E   A B O U T ▲

We'll cover files in Chapter 2, so be patient.

For instance, a popular command in UNIXdom is **cat**, one of the most useful UNIX commands available when it comes to combining and editing text. (Again, note the lack of intuitive sense when it came to naming the **cat** command—it's short for *concatenate*, which is a word we all use daily.) In and of itself, however, **cat** won't do too much. **Cat** becomes useful only when you specify a file or files that **cat** should work with. This is true of virtually every UNIX command.

That's why you need to add more information to the average UNIX command arguments in the form of options and filenames. Generally speaking, every UNIX command is constructed like this:

command *option(s) filename(s)*

Why are *option(s)* and *filename(s)* listed in italics? Because they are *variables:* With most commands, you can use any number of options— or no options at all. The same goes for filenames; you can specify one or more, or none.

▼

There's an amazing amount of flexibility when it comes to entering commands, which is both good and bad: Good that you can do many things with commands, but bad because there's more rope for hanging yourself.

There are a few things to remember when working with commands:

▲ When you enter a command, you must type it in lower-case letters.

▲ For the most part, you can add multiple options to a command. There are some exceptions, which should be noted in any good set of UNIX commands.

Most of the rest of this book is concerned with the proper and efficient use of commands. As such, new concepts and how they relate to commands will be introduced throughout the course of this book. However, there's no way that an introductory book like this could cover every single UNIX command. And, to be honest, there's no reason for you to know more than a half-dozen commands by heart; you can do quite well by looking up what you need as you need it, provided you also have a good list of UNIX commands. (Check the Appendix for a listing of recommended works.)

A good place to start illuminating commands is a sample UNIX session, explained from beginning to end. During the course of the session, we'll return to the topic of commands and how they're entered into the system. And the place a UNIX session starts is with the seemingly simple action of logging on the UNIX system.

Commands and This Book

Throughout this book you'll be presented with commands and how to use them. To keep it simple, each time a command is introduced there will be a Command Reference contained within an accompanying table. The format of the Command Reference will be the same no matter what the command: **command** *option(s) filename(s)*

Purpose: A one-line description of the command.

Options: -a Description of the options

▼

▼

Not every option for every command will be listed. There are some options that you're never going to need or use—indeed, the UNIX command set features many of *those* sorts of options—and there's not much use in covering options that you'll never use.

▲ **L E A R N   M O R E   A B O U T** ▲

The first Command Reference is contained in an upcoming section, "Creating a Command Line," and it details what should be a very simple command, **date**, which returns the current time and date. The reality, though, is quite different—as you'll see.

Logging In a System

When you login a UNIX system, you're announcing your presence to the computer and verifying your existence with a password. Why not just sit down at a terminal and begin typing? *Security*.

UNIX is a multiuser operating system, which means that many people have access to the computer system. And UNIX is anti-egalitarian: Differing levels of security mean that access can be limited to a select group of users.

For instance, the accounting department may have access to one set of information and applications, while the engineering department may have access to another set of information and applications. Many of the concepts inundating the UNIX operating system stem from the need for security. Hence the need for annoying login procedures, terminology, and passwords.

▼

Annoying terminology? Yes, unfortunately. You don't have a name; you have a *username* or *logname*. You have an *account* associated with your username, and it contains information about you and is typically set up by a system administrator. And you have a *password*, a word or set of characters unique to you that verifies your existence.

At this point, we're assuming that your system administrator has set up an account for you and assigned you a password.

Workstation owners might not agree with this assumption, but setting up accounts and passwords is unique to every system, and it's not really of interest to every UNIX user. Check your documentation for more information.

In addition, your system administrator or departmental supervisor should walk you through the process of logging in your system.

When you turn on your monitor or boot your computer or touch the keyboard or do whatever you do in the morning as you begin your computing, the first real computing chore you perform will be logging in the UNIX system. How do you know when it's time to login the system? It's simple—your screen will look like Figure 1.6.

```
Big Company, Inc.


login:  |

Password:
```

FIGURE 1.6 A typical login screen

Of course, your system won't feature the same verbiage, unless you work for a very oddly named company. The system administrator has the ability to change the specific verbiage, and very often UNIX vendors will insert their own little advertising message—as if you really care which UNIX vendor has created the version of UNIX you're using. However, the concept will be the same: You provide a logname and a password. The process goes something like this:

▲ When the system displays **login:**, type in your username in lowercase letters, and then press the **Enter** (or **Return**) key.

▲ When the system displays **password:**, type in your password exactly as it was given to you by the system administrator, and then press the **Enter** (or **Return**) key.

As mentioned, the entire login system exists to enhance system security. This is reflected during the seemingly routine process of logging in the system. When you type in your logname after the **login:** prompt, the characters that you type will appear on the screen—just as you would expect. However, when you type in the characters after the **password:** prompt, the characters do not appear on the screen. The reason is simple: No one looking over your shoulder can read your password and steal it for nefarious purposes.

Of course, not every system is as secure as it should be; for instance, many systems do not require the use of a password. And in some situations a password isn't needed, as in the case of single-user workstations where there's little need for security.

Reality Check: Logging In a System

If you should have trouble logging in a UNIX system, there are a few steps you can take to solve the problem:

▲ If you make a mistake when typing in the username or password, you can either use the **BackSpace** (or **BkSp**) key to go back and reenter the correct letter. Or you can take the lazy approach: Go ahead and enter the incorrect information, knowing full well that the system will tell you your login was incorrect. In this instance, the system will ask you to login again.

▲ If the system tells you that your login was incorrect (or something to that effect; for reasons of security, UNIX systems tend to be somewhat vague when it comes to explanations of why logins fail), it will also give you a chance to reenter a username and password. If the second try also fails, check with your system administrator and make sure you're using the correct username and password.

▲ If the username and password are seemingly accepted by the system and then nothing happens, be patient; UNIX systems can sometimes be balky during times of high workloads. If you've waited a few minutes and nothing happens, check with others around you to see if their systems are working before calling to complain to your system administrator.

The UNIX Shell and Prompt

What happens after you've logged on the UNIX system is largely up to the system administrator. Some systems are set up to go directly into an application. Some systems are set up to open a *graphical interface*. Other systems are set up to show a minimal *text-based display*. Stylistically, the latter two couldn't be more different, as shown in Figures 1.7 and 1.8.

FIGURE 1.7 A typical screen on a text-based terminal

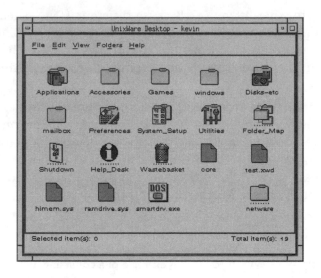

FIGURE 1.8 UNIX with a graphical interface

Both styles, unfortunately, are confusing in different ways. In Figure 1.7, the challenge isn't finding where the command goes—it's finding out what to type in. In Figure 1.8, the challenge is finding exactly where to enter the command.

UNIX features a rather cryptic tool called the *command prompt*, which (unfortunately) assumes a certain level of computing knowledge on your part. Whether by itself on a screen or surrounded by a window on a graphical interface, the command prompt very often is your only access to the operating system. The prompt tells you that the system is ready to accept a command. Depending on the version of UNIX you're using, the command prompt will look something like this:

```
$
```

or

```
%
```

or even

```
Type here, stupid!
```

▼

Why the difference? Because different UNIX shells use different prompts. In addition, both users and system administrators can change prompts to display a custom message, which clearly was the case in the third example of a prompt. But we're getting a little ahead of ourselves here.

Finding the command prompt in Figure 1.7 isn't exactly a difficult proposition, obviously—heck, it's the only thing on the screen. If you're working on a UNIX system that features a graphical interface, the command prompt will be contained in a window labeled **xterm**. Take a look at Figure 1.8 again; you'll see that a window on the right side of the figure features *xterm* on the top.

Both examples use the dollar sign (**$**) as the prompt. This will be also be the case in examples throughout the rest of this book.

When you see an example of a command and a command prompt, remember that you are to type in the command, *not* the command prompt. For instance, if there's an example like:

$ ls -1

you should type only the characters *ls -1*, not the dollar sign or the space following the dollar sign.

Reality Check: Working on a Closed System

After logging in your system, you may find that a program appears immediately on your screen, and that you are limited to working only with that program. There's no way to quit the program and to access the operating system—in these cases quitting the program often logs you off the system.

Many UNIX systems, as a matter of fact, don't allow end users access to the operating system via the command prompt. The goal of these systems is to present an intentionally limited environment, as users tend to cause problems for system administrators when they have access to the operating system—as in asking too many questions and wanting to perform tasks outside the program's capabilities. And life for many users is made much simpler when they don't have access to the operating system—they can work on their chief program and not worry about all the baggage that accompanies multiple applications and the command prompt.

If this is the case in your company, talk with your system administrator and ask for access to a command prompt.

Correcting Mistakes

Typing errors are common for computer users of all sorts, so expect to make a few when you type in UNIX commands. If you do, it's important to remember that there's not much damage you can do to a typical UNIX system, especially if you mistype a command. For instance, you may mistakenly think that there's a command named **tom**. If you were to enter this at a prompt, you'd see the following:

```
$ tom
tom not found
$
```

This is called an *error message*. It's not exactly a serious matter—as you can see, the worse thing to happen was to burn off a few computing cycles. Don't worry too much about error messages if you know that you've mistyped a command line.

However, if you're an extremely fastidious and fussy computer user, you can make changes to command lines in the midst of typing them. Let's say you want to enter a command named **cat**, but you mistype and enter the following instead:

```
$ can
```

Before you hit the **Return** key, you decide you want to go back and delete the *n*, replacing it with *t*.

At this point, look for one of several characters on your keyboard used to delete the preceding character: **Backspace**, **BkSp**, or ←. If you press the key once, the cursor will appear to move over the top of the *n*, but the *n* will continue to appear on the screen. Don't worry—this is normal. Go ahead and type the *t* needed to complete the command, and then type the **Return** key.

Error messages become more serious when there's actually something wrong with the system. Typically, there are many reasons for error messages, and they are all specific to the error message. Because of this, you won't cover error messages at once, but rather in the context of your normal computing chores, as detailed throughout this book.

Putting Them Together: The Command Line

As stated earlier, a command needs something to operate with. When you specify a file to be used with the **cat** command, you're creating a *command line*, which consists of a command (or commands) along with any additional arguments.

Flash back to our initial discussion of commands and the construction of a typical command:

command *option(s) filename(s)*

A command line can consist of a single command, with appropriate options and filenames. However—and here's where UNIX can be extremely confusing for the beginner—a command line can also feature more than one command.

More than one command? Yes. The commands don't need to relate to one another, as a matter of fact; you can send two commands to the system at one time. In this instance, the system will process the commands in the order they are presented. A common command line features a command performing an action, with the results being sent to the printer, as we'll see in the following two sections.

There are some things to remember when putting together a command line:

▲ Commands must be entered in lowercase letters. However, case matters when it comes to options and filenames. In UNIX commands, the options *-a* and *-A* can mean two different things. And the case counts when specifying filenames: **Kevin**, **KEVIN**, and **kevin** would be treated by the system as three different filenames.

▲ Options must always be listed before filenames.

▲ You must use spaces between the elements of a command line.

▲ If you put two unrelated commands on a command line, you must separate them with a semicolon (;), with the construction something like:

command1 *option(s) filename(s);* **command2** *option(s) filename(s)*

Creating a Command Line

Now that you know all there is to know about commands and command lines (fat chance, right?), you may want to experiment with a few commands. Here, we'll assume that you're already logged in the system and know where the prompt is located.

You can start with the most basic and worthless of UNIX commands, **date**. This command lists what date the computer thinks it is. There's no way for the computer to know absolutely what date and time it is, of course. It can only work with information provided by the system administrator. If the system administrator provides bad information, the system will spew out bad dates and times. Such is the way of all computing adventures.

▼

```
$ date
```

After you type **Return** at the end of the command line, the system will return what it thinks the date and time is:

```
Sun Mar 13 19:32 CST 1994
```

Admittedly, this is not the most illuminating of examples. There were no options or filenames listed, and the output from the command is of limited worth; you're essentially using a *very* expensive computer system as the equivalent of a $2.99 desk calendar. However, the **date** command does feature an option, as well as the ability to return the time in several different formats. The Command Reference for the **date** command is found in Table 1.1.

If you had any doubts about the complexity and the inconsistency of the UNIX operating system, they should be dispelled by the Command Reference for the **date** command. In theory, the **date** command does only one thing: Return the current time and date. However, there are a number of ways that UNIX can return this information, as shown in the formats listed in Table 1.1—and these aren't even *all* of the formats available. While there is an option associated with the **date** command, you're not very likely to use it, as it returns the time in Greenwich Mean Time—hence its omission from the Command Reference. And virtually no other UNIX command feature *formats* as part of a command line. Other more obscure formats, such as returning the date as a Julian date, have been omitted from Table 1.1.

TABLE 1.1 Command Reference for the date command

> **date +*format***
>
> **PURPOSE**
> The **date** command displays the current date in a wide variety of formats (some of which are listed).

▼

FORMATS

%a	Day of the week abbreviated (Sun, Mon, et al.).
%A	Day of the week spelled out (Sunday, Monday, et al.).
%b	Month abbreviated (Jan, Feb, et al.) (same as **%h**).
%B	Month spelled out (January, February, et al.).
%d	Day of the month in two digits (01-31).
%D	Date returned in *mm/dd/yy* format.
%e	Day of the month as numeral (1-31).
%h	Month abbreviated (Jan, Feb, et al.) (same as **%b.**).
%m	Month returned as a number (01 for January, 02 for February, et al.).
%p	Time of day indicated (AM or PM).
%y	Year returned in two digits (94).
%Y	Year returned in four digits (1994).

Command

A more useful command is **who**, which lists the users currently logged on the system. The information returned by the system will look something like the following:

```
$ who
maryann    term/06    Mar 13    07:32
ginger     term/05    Mar 13    11:12
skipper    term/04    Mar 13    11:45
```

This tells us that users named maryann, ginger, and skipper are currently using the system, as well as the times they logged on. The Command Reference for the **who** command is listed in Table 1.2.

▼

TABLE 1.2 COMMAND REFERENCE FOR THE WHO COMMAND

who *options file*

PURPOSE

The **who** command shows the names and other information about other users logged on the system.

OPTIONS

am I	Displays who you are (your system name).
-a	Uses all available options.
-H	Inserts column headings.
-q	Quick who; displays only usernames.
-s	Returns name, line, and time fields (default).

Reality Check: What To Do If Your System Freezes

No computer system is foolproof, and that's certainly true of a UNIX system. You can't imagine the complexity involving the average UNIX system—indeed, you don't *want* to imagine this complexity—and quite honestly there are a lot of things that can go wrong. Virtually all of these things are totally unrelated to you or any action that you could take.

Still, there's a pretty good chance you'll be rolling along in your work and run into the situation where the computer stops responding to your actions, or only partially responds to your actions. If this happens, just stop and wait a few minutes. When a UNIX system gets too busy, it will stop responding to every user and devote its energies to important tasks.

If after a few minutes the system won't respond to anything you do, then you've got some bigger problems. Depending on how the system responds to your frantic keystrokes, there are things you can do:

▲ Press the **Return** key. It's common for beginning users to forget to type the **Return** key after entering a command line. And it's not uncommon for experienced users to forget to type the **Return** key after entering a command line.

▲ Type **Ctrl-Q**. You may have inadvertently stopped a program by typing **Ctrl-S**. This key combination will restart the program.

▲ Type **Ctrl-Z**. You don't need to know why at this point of your UNIX education. Just do it.

▲ If the system accepts your keystrokes but ignores the **Return** key, type **Ctrl-J** instead of **Return**.

However, after all of this rigmarole, there's the good chance that the system is still ignoring you. In this instance, punt—go and tell your system administrator that you've got a problem that needs some expert assistance.

Logging Out

At the end of the day, it's considered good etiquette to log off the system, rather than just walking away from your terminal or turning off the monitor. Logging off prevents someone else from sitting down at your terminal and committing unspeakable acts (remember: security), and it also reduces the work performed by a computer system, since the system must keep track of every user logged on the system.

Your exact actions when logging off the system will depend on your system configuration. Generally speaking, however, to log off the system, you can enter one of the following commands:

```
$ exit
```

or

```
$ logout
```

At this point, the **login:** prompt should reappear on the screen for the vast majority of users.

▼

Reality Check: Logging Out

Nothing in UNIX is ever easy, and that includes the seemingly simple act of ending your work day by logging off the system.

For instance, if you've been working with a graphical interface, generally speaking you're going to have to close all of the windows before you can walk away from the terminal. This doesn't require a tremendous effort, granted, but it still can be considered more complex than necessary.

Similarly, the system may not *allow* you to log off. Though we're getting a little ahead of ourselves here, there are situations where you can start programs and then forget about them, but they continue to run in the background.

In this instance, the system will tell you something like:

```
There are stopped jobs.
```

Here, you'll have to start the jobs and end them correctly.

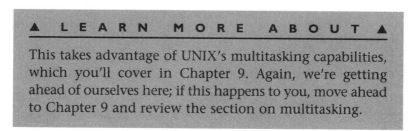

▲   L E A R N   M O R E   A B O U T   ▲

This takes advantage of UNIX's multitasking capabilities, which you'll cover in Chapter 9. Again, we're getting ahead of ourselves here; if this happens to you, move ahead to Chapter 9 and review the section on multitasking.

This Chapter in Review

▲ UNIX is an operating system. As such, it controls every part of the computer, taking your instructions and making sure they are performed by the computer.

▲ These instructions are called commands. There are hundreds of UNIX commands, but there are only a small amount that you'll actually use daily.

▼

▲ Your first command of the day occurs when you log on
the UNIX system, when you announce your presence to
the system with a username and password.

▲ After the system knows you're logged on, you'll either
begin work directly within a program, or else you'll be
able to enter commands directly at a command prompt.

▲ The location of the command prompt will depend on
what type of UNIX you are using: either at the top of the
screen or contained within a window.

▲ The command prompt allows you to enter commands
along with very precise instructions. These instructions are
unique to each UNIX command and are called arguments.

▲ There are rules to follow when entering commands into
the system. For instance, commands are entered in lowercase letters, while arguments can be in either uppercase
or lowercase letters.

▲ The combination of commands and arguments is called
a command line. Creating a command line can be as
simple as entering a command with no arguments, or as
complex as you want, featuring multiple commands and
multiple arguments.

▲ At the end of the day, it's considered good form to log
off the system. To do so, you'll type **exit** or **logout** at the
command prompt.

▪ CHAPTER TWO ▪
File and Directory Basics

Most of your daily interaction with the UNIX operating system will center around the use of files and directories—tools that you'll use to store information. Topics in this chapter include:

- ▲ What a file is, and why it is important.
- ▲ File basics and file types.
- ▲ File and directory names.
- ▲ The home directory and storing your work.
- ▲ Rules when naming files.
- ▲ The current directory, and changing it.
- ▲ Absolute and relative pathnames.
- ▲ File navigation tools, such as **cd** and **pwd.**
- ▲ Listing files and directories with the **ls** command.
- ▲ Viewing file permissions with the **ls** command.
- ▲ Setting file permissions with the **chmod** command.
- ▲ Viewing files with the **cat**, **more**, and **pg** commands.

▼

What is a File, and Why is It Important?

Y ou may have noticed something unusual when reading through Chapter 1: There were references to files and filenames, without any definition or explanation. This wasn't an oversight; rather, files are so important within UNIX that they warrant their own chapter, but it takes a little experience with UNIX concepts before any discussion of files becomes relevant. Hence this chapter.

A *file* is the mechanism for storing information on a UNIX system. Without files, there would be no UNIX. The instructions that make up the operating system are contained in a score of files. The information that you type in the system, such as letters and memos, are stored in files. Information about the system itself is stored in files.

You see, everything about, within, and concerning UNIX is contained in files. When you want to print a letter, you call upon printer information contained in a file to make sure the letter is printed. When you want to run a program, you use a file containing the program's information. And the commands discussed in Chapter 1 are all contained within files, as are the commands discussed throughout the rest of this book.

If this sounds a little overwhelming, don't worry about it for now. For the most part, you don't need to know exactly how files work within UNIX; you just need to know how to make files work for you. It's hard enough to keep track of the rules surrounding files and directories—expecting you to remember why most of these rules exist would be unreasonable.

File Basics

A file is represented by a *filename* on the UNIX system. The filename tells the system where to look for information on the computer system's disk storage; the operating system takes this information and organizes it so that you can use it.

This is technical

If you could actually view the contents of a hard disk directly, you'd see a bunch of symbols making little sense to you. The contents of files are represented in bits. Because it would be silly for anyone to expect you to keep track of the 1,048,576 characters in a one-megabyte file, UNIX assigns a filename to the raw lump of data.

A file can contain pretty much anything an application wants it to contain. Database managers, like *Oracle* and *Sybase*, create files with specially formatted data. So do page-layout programs like *FrameMaker*. Again, you don't need to worry about these formats; the applications take care of this for you.

File Types

What you *may* have to worry about is the type of file you're working with. When *Oracle* creates a file, the resulting file is a specific type of file. Similarly, a programmer creates another type of file that ends up as part of a program.

There are four main types of files:

▲   Ordinary files
▲   Directories
▲   Special device files
▲   Links

As a user, you'll use all four types of files almost every day, and you may not even be aware of it. In this chapter, each type of file will be explained. And you'll see how you can command the UNIX system to decipher file types for you.

Ordinary Files

Here is where UNIX jargon actually matches the reality of the situation—an *ordinary file* is just that, rather ordinary in several ways. Essentially, you can think of ordinary files as data files. When *Oracle* or *FrameMaker*

▼

create files, they create ordinary files to store the data. The specific meaning of an ordinary file becomes clearer when you review the specific types of ordinary files:

▲ *Text files* contain ASCII characters. ASCII is a lowest-common-denominator format, containing representations of regular letters and numerals that can be read by virtually every type of computer. If you use a text editor to create a letter and save it as a file, the resulting file will be in ASCII format. An ASCII file created by a UNIX text editor can be read by a *Windows* or Macintosh word processor. A text file contains only the characters you see on your screen.

▲ *Data files* are more complicated than text files, for they contain both the data and how the data is to look and act within an application. For instance: Let's say you create a page using *FrameMaker*, a popular UNIX desktop-publishing program. You create the page, put a headline on the top, and place text on the remainder of the page. The resulting file will contain the text you see on the page, but it will also contain more information about that page: How large the letters are to be when the file is printed, what fonts the letters are, and other information about the layout of the page (margins, columns, etc.).

The same would be true of files created by database-management programs like *Oracle*. If you pull a record from an *Oracle* database and display it on your screen, all you'll see is the specifics of the entry, such as the name, address, and other information. What you won't see is the formatting information contained within the database, or the other entries within the database that aren't displayed.

Why does this matter? A common problem for most users—beginner or intermediate—is realizing that data files contain information specific to an application.

If you tried to read the *Oracle* database information in *FrameMaker* or another UNIX application, you'd get either an error message or a screen full of gibberish. Similarly, a text editor made to work only with ASCII characters would choke on a file created in *FrameMaker*. Application-specific information creates problems in other applications. So while it seems logical that information you type into *Oracle* should be accessible in a text editor, it doesn't work this way.

▲ *Command text files* are like text files, but there's one big difference: They are meant to be used by the UNIX system to perform specific actions.

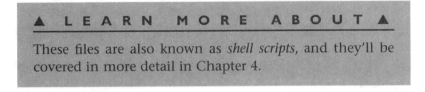

▲ **L E A R N   M O R E   A B O U T** ▲

These files are also known as *shell scripts*, and they'll be covered in more detail in Chapter 4.

▲ *Executable files* are programs created by programmers. If you try to read an executable file with any application, you'll generate more than a few error messages. There are quite a few executable files within UNIX—remember, UNIX commands are nothing more than executable files. You've already covered commands in Chapter 1.

Directories

Directories organize files. Directories contain all pertinent information about a file: its name, its permissions, the date it was created, its type, and more.

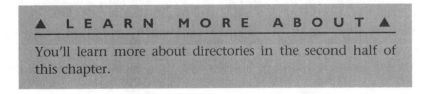

▲ **L E A R N   M O R E   A B O U T** ▲

You'll learn more about directories in the second half of this chapter.

▼

Special Device Files

Special device files contain information about the different physical parts of the UNIX system. For instance, the printer connected to your UNIX system is represented by a special device file, as is your terminal, your neighbor's terminal, and all of the other terminals connected to the UNIX system.

This setup allows changes to be made easily to the UNIX system. For instance: If your system administrator were to connect a nice laser-printer to the UNIX system and replace that grungy old dot-matrix printer, the only change to the system would be the changing of the device file that represents the system's printer.

You won't need to use device files very often, so don't worry too much about them. Generally, device files are set up by the system administrator to be bulletproof to changes from users—you'll be able to read the file and use it, but not make changes to it. If you want to print a file, just worry about the specific commands for printing that file. not the process.

Links

Links represent one of the more ingenious aspects of the UNIX operating system. Though you won't have to worry too much about linking files, an explanation of links illuminates how UNIX systems work.

Computer hardware is expensive, especially when you're talking about hardware needed to support 50 or more users. Particularly expensive are disk drives to store all the information generated by these users, as well as the disk space needed by the UNIX operating system itself.

In order to use as little disk space as possible, *links* are utilized. A link is actually another name for an existing file located elsewhere on the system. Very often a file you use will also be used by another user on the system. The file may be a UNIX program or it could contain company information. Instead of having two separate files taking up precious disk real estate, UNIX allows two or more users to share the file by creating links to the file.

On older UNIX systems, links had to occur between two files residing on the same filesystem. The newest version of UNIX includes *symbolic links*, which allow files from two different filesystems to be linked.

Generally speaking, you won't need to worry about whether a link is symbolic or not.

Determining File Type

When will you need to know the difference between file types? Anytime you're working with files, essentially. Knowing that a file is an executable file, as opposed to a data file, can be useful information when you're looking for a file and you're not quite sure of the name. In addition, the knowledge that a file is executable will also let you know what programs you have on your system.

You may be wondering exactly how you determine the file type. The answer is simple: By listing the files in your directory with the **ls** command.

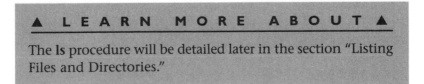

▲ L E A R N   M O R E   A B O U T ▲

The **ls** procedure will be detailed later in the section "Listing Files and Directories."

File and Directory Names

Because everything in UNIX is represented by a file, it also stands to reason that a large UNIX system, used by hundreds of users, could contain tens of thousands of files. Obviously, there needs to be a way to organize this potentially humungous number of files, as well as make sure that files containing sensitive data—such as payroll information—are seen only by the appropriate workers.

UNIX allows for *directories*, used to group files. A directory itself is only a file containing the names of other files (following the UNIX practice of making *everything* within the system a file). The system looks inside of these files in order to find information about the file in question.

Figuring out how UNIX organizes directories can be a complicated task for the beginner, as UNIX isn't very friendly when it comes to information about directories. And while the directory system may be logical for a system administrator or computer scientist, this logic isn't apparent to the beginning user.

Take a look at Figure 2.1. This is a drawing that represents the hierarchy of a UNIX directory system.

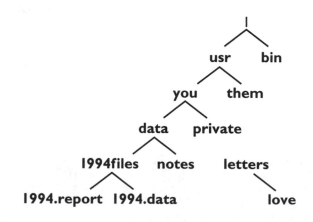

Figure 2.1 A portion of a UNIX directory structure

A directory structure is often compared to a family tree. At the top of the family tree you have the directory that holds all other directories. In UNIX parlance, this directory is the *root directory* and is represented by a slash (/). Figure 2.1 uses lines to indicate the relationships between directories. For instance, the root directory (/) contains two other directories, **usr** and **bin**, which are *subdirectorie*s of the root directory.

Any directory that is contained within another directory is called a subdirectory. Every UNIX directory—except the root directory—is a subdirectory of another directory.

Going down the family tree, you can see that usr contains two additional directories, **you** and **them**, while the directory **you** contains the subdirectories **data** and **private**, and so on. Looking at the directory tree from the ground up, the directory **you** is said to be the *parent directory* of the **data** subdirectory.

Generally speaking, a directory tree won't be as simple as this example; for instance, the root directory (/) usually contains at least six or seven subdirectories, and these subdirectories will hold tens or even hundreds of their own subdirectories. This is why wading through a UNIX file system is sometimes a very scary notion, particularly in a big company with lots of employees. However, there is usually some semblance of order to a UNIX filesystem.

This is technical

Almost every UNIX system contains four or five basic directories, such as **tmp**, **bin**, and **usr**. Even so, their usage is not universal; many UNIX systems don't have a directory named **users**, but may instead have a directory called **u** or **home**.

Your system may have a tool for displaying a UNIX filesystem, especially if your system features a graphical interface. For instance, *UnixWare* contains a handy utility for displaying files and directories, as shown in Figure 2.2.

▼

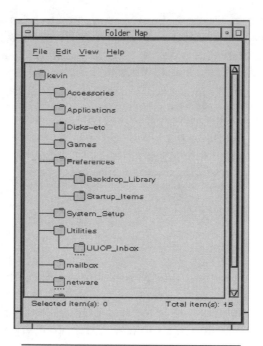

Figure 2.2 The UnixWare file browser

If your system lacks a file browser, you'll have to tackle file management the old-fashioned way: by using the UNIX command line. The rest of this chapter covers file management through the command line, but the principles should apply even if you're using a file browser.

The Home Directory

When you login a UNIX system, you're placed at a specific point in the directory structure. This is called your **home directory**, and it contains most of the files that define your UNIX usage. Users, as well as files, must exist within a directory. In theory, this directory contains the files you need to complete your work. This might include letters and memos, as well as the files that define your personal usage.

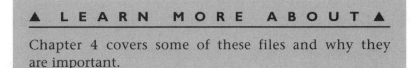

▲ L E A R N   M O R E   A B O U T ▲

Chapter 4 covers some of these files and why they are important.

For now, it's more important to know that your home directory is the place for you to store your work files.

A directory can be likened to a drawer in a file cabinet. Inside of the drawer are several file folders. Since a directory is nothing more than a file that contains the filenames of other files, you can think of your home directory as your personal drawer in the UNIX filesystem.

The idea is to organize these files in an orderly fashion. Take a peek at Figure 2.1 again. Within the directory named **you** there are two subdirectories, **data** and **private**. Within the directory **data** are two subdirectories, **1994files** and **notes**, while the subdirectory **letters** is within the **private** directory. The intent here, obviously, is to separate personal correspondence from corporate correspondence. The philosophy can be extended to other categories of files; for instance, electronic-mail messages from fellow employees can be filed in a directory named **email**, while memos from your boss can be filed in a directory named **memos**.

Don't worry about creating too many subdirectories: The UNIX system doesn't place many limits on the number of subdirectories you produce.

Paying attention to how your files are organized is one the real tricks of efficient UNIX usage: You'll be surprised how many files you end up creating over a few months, and you'll also be surprised to see how quickly you forget about most of them. This is also why it's important to be careful about how you name files. There's no required link between the contents of the file and the filename. For instance, a

▼

file containing a list of apple trees could be called **oranges**. Or a file containing a list of customers could be called **suckers**.

The unwritten rule, however, says that the contents of a file should correspond somewhat to the filename. Programmers work with some specific rules containing filenames, as do database-management experts. And so should you, if you want to keep track of the many UNIX files you'll end up generating in the course of your daily work.

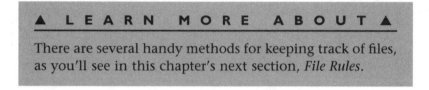

▲ **L E A R N   M O R E   A B O U T** ▲

There are several handy methods for keeping track of files, as you'll see in this chapter's next section, *File Rules*.

There are a few simple things you can do when naming files to help you keep track of them. Refer again to Figure 2.1, and you'll see that the directory **1994files** contains two files, **1994.report** and **1994.data**. Placing a date somewhere in a file is a good tool for making sure that filenames are individualistic—when it comes to routine correspondence, you can place the date somewhere in the filename, such as **memo.612** or **letters.1212**.

File Rules

Remember the following rules when you're naming files:

▲ *A filename can be up to 14 characters in length, generally speaking*. This isn't true across the board—the newest implementation of UNIX, System V Release 4, allows for unlimited lengths—but it's still a good rule to follow, even if your specific system allows for more than 14 characters. Why? Because you'll probably be typing filename into your system often, and long filenames are a pain to type, as well as being more prone to causing typing errors on your part.

▲ *You must be specific about the case of the letters in the filename.* In UNIX, the following three filenames would be considered different files:

```
Kevin
KEVIN
kevin
```

Very often beginners get frustrated by this rule. They may be typing the correct filename, only to discover that the system is denying access because a few letter cases are incorrect.

▲ *A filename is one word, with no spaces between.* UNIX uses spaces on a command line to break down the line into logical segments. Because of this, a filename can only be one word, without any spaces within the filename. (By contrast, the Macintosh allows spaces in filenames.) For instance, the following filename would be rejected by UNIX:

```
kevin report
```

That's a shame, since most of us learned to anticipate spaces between words when we learned to read. A name like *kevin report* is definitely a lot easier to pick out of a list than *kevinreport.*

Because spaces help us pick filenames out of lists, the UNIX community responded to the problem by inserting the underscore (_) character between words. To the eye, there's a space between the words. To the system, there's a character between the two portions of a single word:

```
kevin_report
```

▲ ***Not all keyboard characters can be used in a filename***. This is a matter of convention, not due to a limitation imposed by UNIX. (On a large system, you'll more than likely cause some problems if you use the following characters. So don't.) The frowned-upon characters are:

! @ # $ % ^ & ( ) [ ] ' " ? \ | ; < > 1` + -

▲ ***You can place a period anywhere in a filename***. Other operating systems, most notably DOS, requires that a filename be limited to eight characters, followed by a period and an extension. UNIX is more flexible; a period can be anywhere.

Your Files

Since everything concerning UNIX is contained in a file, it also follows logically that information about *you* is stored within a file. UNIX doesn't know you from Mark Twain when you sit down and login at a terminal. When you enter your username, you're telling the UNIX system who you are, verifying that information with a password. The system then takes that information to look up information about you in several files.

There's no secret as to the identity of these files, so don't feel like there's some hidden information about you lurking within the system. However, many of these files are hidden; that is, they can't be seen via normal file-management tools unless you explicitly look for them.

Any file beginning with a period (.) is considered to be hidden by the UNIX operating system. Still, you have access to these files, and by changing these files, you can change the way you use UNIX.

▲ **L E A R N   M O R E   A B O U T** ▲

Changing hidden files will be covered in more detail in
Chapter 4.

The Current Directory

Like files and directories, a user must occupy a position on the directory
tree. As you learned earlier in this chapter, when you login a UNIX
system, you're placed in your home directory. At that point, the home
directory is also your **current** directory (also referred to as your **working**
directory). It is from this point in the UNIX filesystem that you perform
your tasks.

However, not all of the files you need will be contained in your
current directory. There will be many instances where you'll need to
move around the UNIX filesystem and change your current directory.

The UNIX command **cd** (short for *change* directory) does
just that—changes your current directory. It's a simple
command, as you'll see in the Command Reference listed
in Table 2.1, and its syntax is very simple:

`cd directory`

where *directory* is the name of the new current directory.

▼

TABLE 2.1 COMMAND REFERENCE FOR THE CD COMMAND

cd *directory*

PURPOSE
The **cd** command changes the current directory to a new directory.

OPTIONS
None.

Take Your time

Before you learn how to use the **cd** command, you'll need to learn about pathnames—both absolute and relative. As a matter of fact, you'll learn a lot more about the **cd** command as you learn about pathnames.

Absolute Pathnames

If you take a look at Figure 2.1 again, you'll see that the UNIX file-system—as portrayed in this illustration—looks somewhat like an inverted tree, with branches shooting from the **root** directory.

If you were to follow the lineage of the file **1994.report**, which you can find at the bottom of the tree structure, you'd see that it is within a series of directories, in a direct line to the **root** directory. If you were to list this path, the result would be **/usr/you/data/1994files/1994.report**. This is the file's *absolute pathname*.

At first glance, an absolute pathname looks confusing. However, if you were to break apart the portions of the absolute pathname, you'd see that it makes sense:

▲ The **root** directory always begins an absolute pathname and is represented by the first slash (/).

▲ A move down the directory tree is represented by another slash (/).

▲ The first subdirectory of the **root** directory is **usr**.

▲ The **you** directory is a subdirectory of **usr**, which in turn is a subdirectory of the **root** directory, represented by the leading slash (/).

▲ The **data** directory is a subdirectory of **you**, which is a subdirectory of usr, which in turn is a subdirectory of the **root** directory, represented by the leading slash (/).

▲ The **1994files** directory is a subdirectory of **data**, which is a subdirectory of **you**, which is a subdirectory of **usr**, which in turn is a subdirectory of the **root** directory, represented by the leading slash (/).

▲ Finally, the **1994.report** is contained within the **1994files** directory, a subdirectory of **data**, which is a subdirectory of **you**, which is a subdirectory of **usr**, which in turn is a subdirectory of the **root** directory, represented by the leading slash (/).

Totally confused? Don't be. Figure 2.3 illustrates the absolute pathname for **/usr/you/data/1994files/1994.report** in a more logical fashion.

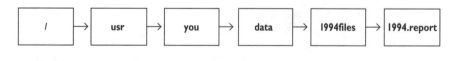

Figure 2.3 The path for the 1994.report file

You'll use this absolute pathname when working with files outside of your home directory. For instance, you may want to verify that the **1994.report** file exists.

You can use the **ls** command (which you'll learn more about later in this chapter). However, the **ls** command works only on the current directory unless you tell it to do otherwise. It is also used to generate a listing for a single file. Putting these two nuggets of information together you can then look for a single file in a directory other than your current directory. The resulting command line would look like this:

```
$ ls /usr/you/data/1994files/1994.report
/usr/you/data/1994files/1994.report
```

Relative Pathnames

Typing out an absolute pathname every time you want to work with a file outside of the current directory is a pain, of course. There's a handy tool within UNIX that will cut down on the potential amount of typing.

A *relative pathname* is just what the name implies—a pathname that's shortened in relationship to your present directory position. A good way to illustrate a relative pathname is to use an example. When you login a UNIX system, you're always placed in your home directory. Look at the directory tree shown in Figure 2.4.

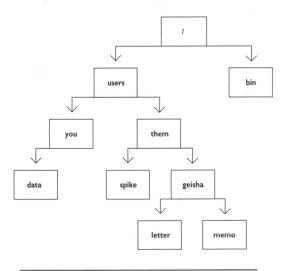

Figure 2.4 Another sample directory tree

You remember that absolute filenames begin with a slash (/), indicating that the filename is relative to the root directory (/). When you're working with a lot of directories, typing out absolute pathnames can be a real pain. Instead you can move around the UNIX filesystem by using relative pathnames, in which you specify a file or directory relative to your current position in the UNIX filesystem.

For instance: If your current directory is the **users** directory, the relative pathname to the **you** directory is merely **you**. To make **you** your current directory, use the following command line:

```
$ cd you
```

Similarly, the relative pathname to the **geisha** directory from **users** would be **them/geisha**. Because there's no slash beginning the pathname, UNIX knows that the path is relative to the current directory—in other words, the pathnames start at the current directory, not the **root** directory.

Relative pathnames also work when moving up through the directory tree. UNIX uses two dots (..) as a shorthand for the directory above the current directory.

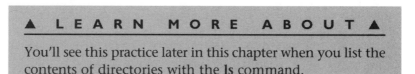

▲ **L E A R N M O R E A B O U T** ▲

You'll see this practice later in this chapter when you list the contents of directories with the **ls** command.

You can use the dots to specify one move up the directory tree, again relative to the current directory.

Again, using Figure 2.4 as an example: **spike** is your current directory, and you want to make **geisha** your current directory. Instead of typing out the cumbersome command line:

```
$ cd /users/them/geisha
```

you can specify the **geisha** directory relative to your current directory:

```
$ cd ../geisha
```

This command tells the system to move up one level on the directory tree (as specified by ..) and then to the subdirectory **geisha** (as specified by /geisha).

UNIX doesn't care if you use absolute or relative pathnames. You can use both within command lines. The key
is accuracy when using either method.

Reality Check: Using Relative Pathnames

A mistake many beginners make—as well as many experienced users—
is assuming that a relative filename can be used all the time. For
instance, why not use the following command line to change the
current directory to **geisha**, since it lists a relative pathname?

```
$ cd them/geisha
```

If you tried this command line, you'd get an error message, saying
that the **them/geisha** directory was not found:

```
$ cd them/geisha
UX:cd: ERROR: them/geisha: Does not exist
```

Indeed, it doesn't exist—at least in the example directory tree
shown in Figure 2.4. The above command line tells the UNIX system
that you want to change your current directory to a *subdirectory* of the
current directory—and **them/geisha** is indeed not a subdirectory of
the current directory. Always remember that when moving up and
down the directory tree and using relative pathnames, you must use
two dots (..) to move *up* the tree.

Navigation Tools

As explained in the section on "The Current Directory," there are
times when you'll want to move around the directory tree, using the **cd**
command. In the previous two sections, you've seen the **cd** command
used in a variety of ways.

There are times when you'll want to know what your current directory is, however. To do so, use the **pwd** command (short for *print working directory*). This simple command, as outlined in Table 2.2, does only one thing—returns the current directory as an absolute pathname:

```
$ pwd
/users/them/geisha
```

TABLE 2.2 COMMAND REFERENCE FOR THE PWD COMMAND

> **pwd**
>
> **PURPOSE**
> The **pwd** command returns the current working directory.
>
> **OPTIONS**
> None.

Listing Files and Directories

Before you do anything with a file or set of files, you need to know exactly what files exist. In UNIX, you can find out practically everything about a file with one handy command, **ls**.

Ls is short for list, and it lists the contents of a directory. It does *not* list the contents of a file, however, as you might expect from a command named *list*. UNIX commands are not quite as logical as UNIX fans would have you believe.

This is both one of the simplest (conceptually, there's nothing more simple than returning the contents of a directory) and complex (witness the presence of 20 options) commands within the UNIX operating system. Of course, out of the 20 options, not all are equal; you'll use *-F* and *-l* quite a bit, while chances are you won't find much use for *-u* or *-c*. Still, a rundown of some of the more useful variations of **ls** will serve to illustrate this handy command, as you'll see in Table 2.3.

TABLE 2.3 COMMAND REFERENCE FOR THE LS COMMAND

ls *options names*

PURPOSE

The **ls** command lists the contents of a directory.

OPTIONS

-1   Lists one item per line.

-a   Lists all contents, including hidden files.

-c   Lists by creation/modification time.

-C   Lists in column (the default on the majority of UNIX systems).

-d   Lists only the name of the directory, not the contents.

-f   Assume that *names* are directories, not files.

-F   Flag executable filenames with an asterisk (*), directories with a slash (/), and symbolic links with @.

-g   Lists in long form (see -l), omitting the owner of the file.

-l   Lists the contents of a directory in long form.

-m   Lists the contents across the screen, separated by commas.

-n   Same as -l, except using numbers instead of names.

-o   Same as -l, except the group name is omitted.

-p   Displays a slash (/) at the end of every directory name.

-q   Lists contents with nonprinting characters represented by a question mark (?).

-r   Lists the contents in reverse order.

-R   Recursively lists the contents of directories.

-s   Lists file sizes in blocks, instead of the default bytes.

-t   Lists the contents in order of time saved, beginning with the most recent.

-x   Lists files in multicolumn format.

Using **ls** by itself on a command line will generate a listing of the contents of the current directory:

```
$ ls
Accessories    Folder_Map   Preferences    Utilities     data
Applications   Games        Shutdown       Wastebasket   mailbox
Disks-etc      Help_Desk    System_Setup   core          netware
```

The columns are listed in alphabetical order (with capital letters listed before lowercase letters), in columnar form. On most UNIX systems, this will be the default. If this is not the default on your system and you want to generate listings in this fashion, use the -C option.

Although you don't know it yet, the usefulness of the above usage of the **ls** command is actually very limited. There's no way to tell what the above files are in terms of directories and files; for all you know, everything returned by the command could be a directory. In addition, the generic **ls** command doesn't list any **hidden** files. UNIX allows the creation of *hidden* files, which are used most often for standard house-keeping tasks by the system and applications.

▲ L E A R N   M O R E   A B O U T ▲

You'll learn about hidden files in Chapter 3 and editing a file called **.profile** in Chapter 4.

Because there are times when you'll need to know about the existence of hidden files, it's a good idea to know how to generate a listing of *all* files. See the difference between the results of the generic **ls** command and the following:

```
$ ls -a
.              .lastsession  .profile      Games         Wastebasket
..             .login        .wastebasket  Help_Desk     core
.Xdefaults     .oliniterr    Accessories   Preferences   data
.dtfclass      .olinitout    Applications  Shutdown      mailbox
.dtinfo        .olinitrc     Disks-etc     System_Setup  netware
.dtprops       .olsetup      Folder_Map    Utilities
```

You'll notice a fair amount of new files generated using the -a option. You'll also notice that the listing leads with . and ... These symbols are used to denote the current (.) directory and the parent (..) directory.

To return information on a specific file or directory, type the name of the file or directory after the **ls** command:

```
$ ls data
data
```

If the file or directory in question was not contained in the current directory, you'd receive an error message like the following:

```
$ ls god
UX:ls: ERROR: Cannot access god: No such file or directory
```

So far the **ls** command has not differentiated between files and directories. To do so, use the *-F* option:

```
$ ls -F
Accessories/    Folder_Map@   Preferences/    Utilities/      data
Applications/   Games/        Shutdown@       Wastebasket@  mailbox/
Disks-etc/      Help_Desk@    System_Setup/   core            netware@
```

Unless you tell it otherwise, the **ls** command will organize listings in a columnar fashion, with order descending through a column and then starting again on the next column. To sort entries across the screen in alphabetical order, use the *-x* option:

```
$ ls -x
Accessories   Applications Disks-etc   Folder_Map    Games
Help_Desk     Preferences  Shutdown    System_Setup  Utilities
Wastebasket   core         data        mailbox       netware
```

You can also combine options. For instance, you could apply both the *-x* and the *-F* options simultaneously:

```
$ ls -xF
Accessories/  Applications/ Disks-etc/  Folder_Map@   Games/
Help_Desk@    Preferences/  Shutdown@   System_Setup/ Utilities/
Wastebasket@  core          data        mailbox/      netware@
```

If you want to separate entries with commas instead of spaces, use the *-m* option:

```
$ ls -m
Accessories, Applications, Disks-etc, Folder_Map, Games, Help_Desk,
Preferences, Shutdown, System_Setup, Utilities, Wastebasket, core,
data, mailbox, netware
```

To return the contents of a directory in reverse order, use the *-r* option:

```
$ ls -r
netware    core          System_Setup   Help_Desk     Disks-etc
mailbox    Wastebasket   Shutdown       Games         Applications
data       Utilities     Preferences    Folder_Map    Accessories
```

To list the entries recursively—that is, to list the contents of the directories—use the *-R* option:

```
$ ls -R
./Accessories:
Calculator Clock Mail Terminal Text_Editor

./Applications:
DOS Fingertip_Lib Win Win_Setup

./Disks-etc:
Disk_A Disk_B cdrom1

./Games:
Puzzle Xtetris

./Preferences:
Backdrop_Library      Icons         Miscellaneous Startup_Items
Color                 Keyboard      Mouse
Desktop               Locale        ScreenLock

./Preferences/Backdrop_Library:
Backdrop_Items aztec.gif owl.gif tallship.gif

./Preferences/Backdrop_Library/Backdrop_Items:

./Preferences/Startup_Items:
ScreenLock

./System_Setup:
Appl-n_Setup   Font_Setup    MHS_Setup        Printer_Setup
Dialup_Setup   Icon_Setup    NetWare_Setup    Terminal_Setup
Extra_Admin    Install_Server Password_Setup  User_Setup

./Utilities:
Backup-Restore     System_Status    UUCP_Inbox
NetWare_Access     Task_Scheduler

./mailbox:
```

As you can tell by the use of the *-R* option, there's the potential to generate a ton of information by using the **ls** command. Indeed, UNIX maintains a lot of information about each file—much more than the limited information you've generated so far. If you want to actually see all of this information—and there are definitely times where that is appropriate, as you'll see during a discussion of file permissions—use the *-l* (for *long*) option:

```
$ ls -l
total 2060
drwxr-xr-x   2 kevin  other  1024     Apr 29  21:23  Accessories
drwxr-xr-x   2 kevin  other  1024     Apr 29  21:23  Applications
drwxr-xr-x   2 kevin  other  96       May 1   10:23  Disks-etc
lrwxrwxrwx   1 kevin  other  25       Apr 29  21:23  Folder_Map
drwxr-xr-x   2 kevin  other  96       Apr 29  21:23  Games
lrwxrwxrwx   1 kevin  other  24       Apr 29  21:23  Help_Desk
drwxr-xr-x   4 kevin  other  1024     Apr 29  21:23  Preferences
lrwxrwxrwx   1 kevin  other  23       Apr 29  21:23  Shutdown
drwxr-xr-x   2 kevin  other  1024     Apr 29  21:23  System_Setup
drwxr-xr-x   2 kevin  other  1024     Apr 29  21:23  Utilities
lrwxrwxrwx   1 kevin  other  28       Apr 29  21:23  Wastebasket
-rw-r-r—     1 kevin  other  1048576  Apr 30  11:50  core
-rw-r-r—     1 kevin  other  144      May 1   10:30  data
drwxr-x—-    2 kevin  other  96       Apr 29  21:23  mailbox
lrwxrwxrwx   1 kevin  other  9        Apr 29  21:23  netware
```

Don't be so quick to use the *-l* option by itself, unless you're working on a smaller UNIX system. If you're working on a larger filesystem containing thousands and thousands of files, you may want to consider redirecting the output of the **ls** command to a file.

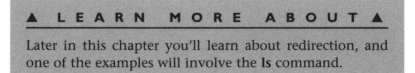

▲ **L E A R N   M O R E   A B O U T** ▲

Later in this chapter you'll learn about redirection, and one of the examples will involve the **ls** command.

▼

The long listing above begins with a summary of the disk space *(2060)* used by the directory, as measured in blocks.

This is technical

A block is usually 4,096 bytes, but this isn't a uniform measure across UNIXdom.

By looking at a specific line in the listing you can see exactly what information is returned by the **ls -l** command line:

```
drwxr-xr-x 2 kevin other  1024 Apr 29 21:23 Accessories
```

And by breaking down this line in reverse order (that is, right to left), the information associated with files should be made clearer.

The first column in our right-to-left explanation contains the files and directories in alphabetical order—in this case, `Accessories`. Because UNIX uses an ASCII-based alphabetization scheme, all of the uppercase letters appear at the beginning of a listing, followed by the lowercase letters. In such a listing, a file named **Zebra** would be alphabetized before a file named **alphabet**, because of the uppercase *Z* and the lowercase a.

Take Your time

Don't worry—you won't need to remember this explanation at any point in your UNIX usage.

The second and third columns (`Apr 29 21:23`) list the date and time the file was created or last changed.

The fourth column (`1024`) records the size of the file, or the amount of disk space it occupies, in bytes.

Bits, Bytes, Kilobytes, and Megabytes

The computer world doesn't measure things in the same manner as the rest of the world. Take, for example, the rather confusing measures of file sizes—bits, bytes, kilobytes, and megabytes. A bit is the most basic measurement found in computing and is either 0 or 1 for a simple reason: The computer, on a base level, sees everything on an either/or basis. However, you'll never work with individual bits during the course of your computing experience. The smallest measure that you'll need to note is a byte (pronounced *bite*), which is eight contiguous bits. It is essentially a single character—the letter *a*, for example, is represented by a single byte. The next measurement is the kilobyte (K), and above that is the megabyte (MB). However, explaining these measurements is not as simple a matter as you might think.

In many of the files listed by the *-l* option, the size of the file is returned as 1,024. That's a magical number in the computer world, as 1,024 bytes equals a kilobyte. This is not a mistake: Because computers process binary information, measurements like kilobytes and megabytes (and gigabytes and terabytes, if you're working with very large filesystems) in powers of 2. Therefore, 2^{10} equals 1,024 (which gives us a kilobyte) and 2^{20} equals 1,048,576 (which gives us a megabyte). The use of *kilo-* and *mega-* in this situation is misleading, since their use has nothing to do with metrics.

And, to be honest, there are very few instances where you'll need to know that a kilobyte is precisely 1,024 bytes, as opposed to around 1,000 bytes. However, it does help explain the recurring instance of 1,024 bytes: many applications create files with a minimum size of 1 kilobyte—and when this measurement is translated to bytes, you end up with the magical 1,024.

The fifth column lists the group that the file belongs to.

Groups will be discussed later in this book, so don't worry about them at the moment.

The sixth column lists the owner of the file. If you owned the file, your login name or username (which you learned about in Chapter 1) is listed here. (If you create a file, you are assumed to own that file.)

The seventh column is the link count, which lists how many files are symbolically linked to the file, or, in the case of directories, how many subdirectories are contained within it, plus two—one for the directory itself, one for the **parent** directory. The minimum number for a directory is two (unless you have a **root** directory with no subdirectories—a highly unlikely occurrence), and that's exactly what we have in our example listing.

The first column—when reading left-to-right—contains what looks like a chaotic set of characters (`-drwxr-xr-x`). However, armed with knowledge, we can summon forth order from the chaos and parse the confusing string of characters, as shown in Figure 2.5.

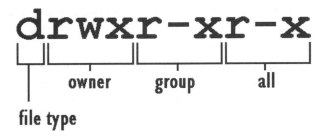

Figure 2.5 File permissions parsed

This contents of this column, `drwxr-xr-x`, is actually four separate sections. The first character represents the file type—a concept covered in the earlier section, "File Types." UNIX uses a single letter to represent the file type, and these letters are listed in Table 2.4.

TABLE 2.4 FILE TYPES LISTED WITH THE -L OPTION

CHARACTER	FILE TYPE
-	Ordinary file.
b	Special block file.
c	Special character file.
d	Directory.
l	Link.
p	Named pipe special file.

For most of your computing needs, you'll only need to worry about directories (d), links (l), and ordinary files (-).

Applying this information to our listing, we can see that the **Accessories** file is actually a directory.

Permissions

The rest of the column concerns the permissions associated with the listing. As a multiuser operating system that must simultaneously serve the needs of a potentially large number of users, UNIX must also have safeguards to ensure that every user can keep some data private— or, in reality, semiprivate.

UNIX provides a basic level of security through **permissions**, which dictate who can do what to a file—no matter if the file is an actual file, a directory, or a program. There are three levels of permissions associated with files:

▲   **Read**, where you can read the file.

▲   **Write**, where you can change the file.

▲   **Execute**, where you can run the file as a program (provided it's an executable file, of course).

Permissions differ slightly when it comes to directories:

▲   **Read**, where you can list the contents of the directory.

▲   **Write**, where you can make or delete files or subdirectories within the directory.

▲   **Execute**, where you can make the directory your current directory using the **cd** command.

By applying these guidelines to the parsed permissions information contained in Figure 2.5 as well as to an example file listing, you can learn a lot about permissions and how they apply to directories. As you can see in Figure 2.5, the permissions can be divided into four distinct sections. The first section, which you have already covered, covers the file type—and you already know that the file is actually a directory.

The second portion of the listing concerns the permissions for the owner of the directory, *rwx*. You'll recall that the owner of this file is *kevin*, and as such the user *kevin* can read (*r*), write (*w*), and execute (*x*) the directory.

The third portion of the listing, *r-x*, concerns the permissions for the group named *other*. This group can read (*r*) and execute the directory (*x*), but cannot write to the directory (-). Permissions are noted in either/or fashion—a user can either read/write/execute a file or directory (*rwx*) or not (-).

The fourth portion of the listing, *r-x*, concerns the permissions for *all* users of the UNIX system. Anyone can read (*r*) and execute the directory (*x*), but no one else can write to the directory (-).

Using the same format, you can see how permissions relate to files—specifically, the **data** file originating from the usage of the **ls -l** command line:

```
-rw-r—r— 1 kevin other   144 May 1 10:30 data
```

Here the permissions are slightly different than what you saw with the **Accessories** directory. To begin with, the listing in the file-type section, -, shows that the file is an ordinary file.

The second portion of the permissions section, *rw-*, indicates that the owner of the file can read (*r*) or write (*w*) the file, but not execute (-) the file. Why not? For one simple reason: The system knows that the file is an ordinary file and not an executable file—and you can't execute a file that not executable.

The third portion of the section, *r—*, is similar: The members of the group *other* can read (*r*) the file, but cannot write to it or execute it (-). The same goes for the fourth portion of the section, *r—*, which concerns the permissions of all users of the system.

Changing Permissions with chmod

In the previous section, the permissions were represented in *symbolic form*. UNIX, owning up to its reputation as a complex operating system, also represents permissions in *numeric form*, using numerals (as you might expect) to represent the permissions.

The numeric form is actually very convenient when you want to change the permissions using the **chmod** (*change mode*) command. However, be warned that using the **chmod** can be a complex endeavor (as you'll see by browsing through Table 2.5), so it's best to wade through the following examples to try match an example to any changes you may want to make.

TABLE 2.5 COMMAND REFERENCE FOR THE CHMOD COMMAND

chmod *option mode filename(s)*

PURPOSE

The **chmod** command changes the permissions on a file or directory. Only the owner of the file or a privileged user can change the mode of a file. There are two ways to change permissions: Through symbolic or numeric form. The numeric form is used to set absolute permission values, while the symbolic form is used to set values relative to the current value.

OPTION

-R   Recursively changes through subdirectories and files.

Let's say that you want to change the permissions associated with a file named **kevin.report**. You want to make sure that you (the owner) can read, write, and execute the file, but you want the members of your group and the rest of the UNIX users to be able to read the file, and not execute the file or write to it.

The command line to accomplish this would be:

```
$ chmod 744 kevin.report
```

At first glance, this isn't going to make any sense to you. However, the numeral *744* refers to the new modes you want to set for the file **kevin.report**. The *mode* is an octal number in one of the formats listed in Table 2.6.

TABLE 2.6 MODES AND THEIR MEANINGS

NUMERAL	MEANING
400	Owner has read permission.
200	Owner has write permission.
100	Owner has execute permission.
040	Group has read permission.
020	Group has write permission.
010	Group has execute permission.
004	All users have read permission.
002	All users have write permission.
001	All users have execute permission.

To get the permissions you want to change to with the **chmod** command, you add the numbers. For example, 423 means that you, the user, can read the file, users in your group can write the file, and the rest of the world can write and execute the file.

 You usually need read permission to execute a file. Therefore, execute permission without having read permission is pretty worthless.

In the example command line earlier, the value of *744* comes from adding together the mode values in such a manner. The lowest possible value is 000—which means no one can read, write, or execute the file—while the highest-possible value is 777, where everyone can read, write, and execute the file. Here's the exact arithmetic used to arrive at 744 in Table 2.7:

▼

TABLE 2.7

400	Owner has read permission.
200	Owner has write permission.
100	Owner has execute permission.
040	Group has read permission.
004	World has read permission.
———	
744	

The next time you would run a **ls** command on the file (using the long form, of course) **kevin.report**, the permissions would be set as:

```
rwxr–r–
```

You can also use the symbolic form to set permissions. However, there's a slight difference between working with numeric forms and working with symbolic forms: When you're working with numeric form, you're setting the permissions in an absolute fashion, but when you're working with the symbolic form, you're setting the permissions relative to the current permissions. A few examples should make this clear to you.

You want to allow yourself, the owner of the file, to execute the file named **kevin**. The following command line accomplishes this:

```
$ chmod u+x kevin
```

The *u+x* portion of the command line changes the permissions in the following manner:

- ▲ *u* specifies that you want to change the permissions for the user, or the owner of the file.
- ▲ + specifies that you want to add a permission to the current permissions.
- ▲ *x* specifies that the change should be applied to the ability to execute the file.

Similarly, you can use this method to remove permissions. The following command line takes away the ability to execute the file **kevin** from the owner of the file:

```
$ chmod u-x kevin
```

The *u-x* portion of the command line changes the permissions in the following manner:

- ▲ *u* specifies that you want to change the permissions for user, or the owner of the file.
- ▲ - specifies that you want to remove a permission from the current permissions.
- ▲ *x* specifies that the change should be applied to the ability to execute the file.

You can also combine various permissions in the same command line, making sure that the settings are separated by a comma (with no spaces on either side of it). In addition, you can set permissions for more than one set of users in the same mode statement, as shown in the following:

```
$ chmod u+x,go-w file.report
```

This allows the owner of the file **file.report** to execute the file, while removing the permissions of the group and all other users to write to the file.

The various symbols used with the **chmod** command, such as *x* and *g*, are listed in Table 2.8.

TABLE 2.8 SYMBOLS USED WITH THE CHMOD COMMAND

SYMBOL	MEANING
u	User (who actually owns the file).
g	Group.
o	Other.
all	All (this is the default).
+	Add a permission to the current permissions.
-	Remove a permission from the current permissions.
=	Assign an absolute permission irrespective of the current permission.
r	Read.
w	Write.
x	Execute.
l	Mandatory lock during access.

▼

There's a lot more associated with the concept of permissions, but most of it is of interest to system administrators and programmers.

Reality Check: Security

Setting permissions on files is the most rudimentary form of security available on a UNIX system. Unfortunately, there's no such thing as *absolute* security when it comes to file permissions. Even if you set up a permission that allows no one else but the owner of the file to read or write the file, there's one user who isn't affected by these permissions— the *root* or *superuser* of the UNIX system, who is considered a privileged user and has access to pretty much the entire UNIX system. Your system administrator has access to superuser status. If you're storing extremely sensitive material in your UNIX files, it would be a good idea to discuss a more potent security setup with your system administrator.

Looking at Files with cat, more, and pg

Now that you know all about files and how they are stored, there's one more topic to cover: Viewing files.

In the previous chapter, reference was made to the **cat** command, and how useful it is. Designed as a tool for combining files (**cat** is the shortened name for *concatenate*), the **cat** command can also be used to view files in a down-and-dirty fashion. A skim through Table 2.8 will show how extensively **cat** can be used in everyday computing chores.

▲ **L E A R N   M O R E   A B O U T** ▲

There's more to the **cat** command, which will be covered in Chapter 3.

TABLE 2.9 COMMAND REFERENCE FOR THE CAT COMMAND

cat *options file(s)*

PURPOSE

The **cat** command performs several frequently used chores:

▲ Combines several files into a new file (using the > operator).

▲ Appends other files to an existing file (using the >> operator).

▲ Displays a file when no operators are specified.

▲ Copies a file to a new name (using the > operator).

▲ Creates a new text file without the use of a text editor.

OPTIONS

- Used as a substitute for a filename, - allows for keyboard entry to be appended to an existing file; **Ctrl-D** ends the keyboard entry.

-s Silent mode; suppresses information about nonexistent files.

-u Output is unbuffered; default is buffered; displays characters in blocks.

-v Prints nonprinting characters, such as control characters, except for tabs, form feeds, and newlines.

-ve Prints nonprinting characters, such as control characters, except for tabs and form feeds, while newlines appear as dollar signs ($).

-vt Prints nonprinting characters, such as control characters, except for newlines, while tabs appear as ^I and form feeds as ^L.

-vet Prints all nonprinting characters.

On a basic level, the use of the **cat** command is quite simple. To display a file on the screen, you merely combine **cat** with the filename on a command line. To display the file **kevin.memo**, you'd use the following command line:

```
$ cat kevin.memo
```

You can display more than one file at a time, one after another. To display **kevin.report**, followed by **kevin.memo**, you'd use the following command line:

```
$ cat kevin.report kevin.memo
```

If you enter **cat** on a command line and fail to specify a file, you'll be frustrated to find that no matter what you type, your keystrokes are merely displayed on the screen. One of the uses for **cat** involves creating a file from scratch. When you use **cat** without a filename, you're invoking this usage. To end this charade, use **Ctrl-D** to end input.

If you're viewing a longer file with the **cat** command, you may find that the text whizzes by on the screen at an uncomfortably fast rate—fast enough so you won't be able to read it. Because there's no way to control how **cat** displays text, it's best used with shorter files that don't run longer than a screen when displayed.

For longer files, you should use **more** or **pg** to display the files. The **more** command will display a file one screen at a time. It also is more interactive than the **cat** command, in that **more** tells you how much of the file is left to view, and it also allows you to go back to screens you have previously viewed, as well as specify a starting line number for viewing a file. Using the **more** command to read a file named **kevin.file** is a matter of putting together a simple command line:

```
$ more kevin.file
```

However, you'll find that the **more** command is made more useful by invoking the -*d* option, which places short instructions on the bottom of the screen (*very* short instructions—**Enter** to continue, **Delete** to end). A command line using this option would look like:

```
$ more -d kevin.file
```

The full list of options associated with the **more** command are listed in the command's Command Reference, found in Table 2.10.

TABLE 2.10 COMMAND REFERENCE FOR THE MORE COMMAND

more *options file(s)*

PURPOSE

The **more** command displays all or parts of a file one screenful at a time. Type **q** to quit, space bar to continue.

OPTIONS

-c	Clears the screen before displaying the next page of the file. This can be quicker than watching pages scroll by.
-d	Displays a prompt at the bottom of the screen, involving brief instructions.
-f	Wraps text to fit the screen width and judges the page length accordingly.
-l	Ignores formfeeds (^L) at the end of a page.
-r	Displays control characters.
-s	Squeezes; ignore multiple blank lines.
-u	Ignores formatting characteristics like underlined text.
-w	Waits for user input to exit.
-n	Sets window size by *n* lines.
+num	Starts output at line number *num*.

OPTIONS WHEN VIEWING A FILE

f	Go to next full screen.
n	Display next file.
p	Display previous file.
q	Quit.

There's only one problem with the **more** command: It's not available on every UNIX system. However, almost every UNIX system does have a similar command called **pg**, which displays a file one page at a time. (The command also goes by the name **page** on some systems; **pg** and **page** are interchangeable command names.) As shown by the Command Reference for **pg** (in Table 2.11), there are many similarities between **more** and **pg**. However, **more** is a little easier to use than **pg** for beginners.

To use **pg** to view a file named **spike.file**, use the following command line:

```
$ pg spike.file
```

If this file was longer than one screen, you'll see a colon (:) on the bottom of the screen. In this case, you'd enter a command (as listed in Table 2.11), or else you can hit the **Return** key to go to the next screen.

TABLE 2.11 COMMAND REFERENCE FOR THE PG COMMAND

page *options file(s)*

PURPOSE

The **pg** command displays all or parts of a file. Type **q** to quit, space bar to continue.

OPTIONS

-c	Clears the screen before displaying the next page of the file. This can be quicker than watching pages scroll by.
-d	Displays a prompt at the bottom of the screen, involving brief instructions.
-f	Wraps text to fit the screen width and judges the page length accordingly.
-l	Ignores formfeeds (^L) at the end of a page.
-r	Displays control characters.
-s	Squeezes; ignore multiple blank lines.

-u	Ignores formatting characteristics like underlined text.
-w	Waits for user input for exiting.
-n	Sets window size by *n* lines.
+num	Starts output at line number *num*.

OPTIONS DURING FILE VIEWING

f	Go to next full screen.
n	Display next file.
p	Display previous file.
q	Quit.

This Chapter in Review

▲ Everything within the UNIX operating system is a file. Most of your daily UNIX usage involves files. Therefore, it's important for you to have a clear idea of how files function within UNIX.

▲ There are four main types of files within UNIX: ordinary, directories, special device files, and links.

▲ A directory structure is often compared to a family tree. At the top of the family tree is a directory called the **root** directory.

▲ Pathnames indicate the placement of files in the directory structure. Pathnames can be absolute—descending in a straight line from the **root** directory—or relative to the current directory.

▲ To view the contents of a directory, use the **ls** command. This lists all files and directories contained within a given directory. It also returns a lot of information about the specific files and directories, such as the permissions, the time the file was last changed, and the owner of the file.

▲   Permissions control which user can do what to a file or directory. The owner of a file, a group, or all users can read a file, write to a file, and/or execute a file.

▲   Changing file permissions is accomplished through the use of the **chmod** command. However, changing file permissions is a tricky business, and before you change permissions, you may want to read through the **chmod** examples.

▲   You can view files by using the **cat**, **more**, or **pg** commands. Shorter files can be viewed with **cat**, but longer files should be viewed with **more** or **pg**.

▪ CHAPTER THREE ▪
UNIX File Tools

UNIX features several tools designed to further your daily computing chores, including:

- ▲ **cp**, which copies files.
- ▲ **mv**, which moves files from one directory to another.
- ▲ **mv**, which also renames files.
- ▲ **rm**, which removes files from the system.
- ▲ **rmdir**, which removes directories from a system.
- ▲ **grep**, which searches through files for specific information.
- ▲ Two variations on **grep**: **egrep** and **fgrep**.
- ▲ **sort**, which sorts the lines of a file in alphabetical or numeric order.
- ▲ **comm** and **cmp**, which compare files.
- ▲ **diff**, which lists the differences in two different files.
- ▲ **bdiff**, **diff3**, and **sdiff**, which extend the power of the **diff** command.
- ▲ **paste** and **join**, which (predictably enough) pastes and joins files.

▼

UNIX Tools: Small, Sleek, and Elegant

As an operating system, the UNIX you're using is a Darwinian creature, evolving from the needs and wants of users over the course of many, many years. As such, UNIX commands tend to be very specific creatures, performing one precise function, albeit in a number of slightly differing ways.

And because UNIX commands evolved in response to users' needs, there are a *lot* of them. For most of your basic UNIX usage, you'll find that most of your needs are linked to files—removing them, moving them, and so on.

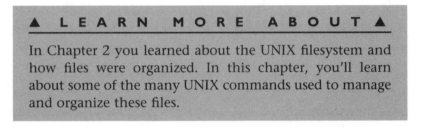

▲ LEARN MORE ABOUT ▲

In Chapter 2 you learned about the UNIX filesystem and how files were organized. In this chapter, you'll learn about some of the many UNIX commands used to manage and organize these files.

For the most part, these are the kinds of commands you'll use most often when you work directly with a UNIX system. These are the tools used to directly work with UNIX files: moving and removing them, cutting and pasting them, and so on. You'll also learn about the options associated with these tools.

Using Cp to Copy Files

Command

The **cp** command is used to copy a file. When you copy a file, the original file remains untouched, and its contents are then copied to the new filename in the new location.

There are many instances where you'll find the **cp** command to be very useful. One of the smartest things you can do is to make copies of your important files. Let's say you were working on an serious corporate project, and you

▼

were storing your work in a file called **stuff**. Since this file is central to your project, you'll want to make sure that you have more than one copy of it on the filesystem, in case the original file is accidentally erased or altered. In this instance, you'd want to use the **cp** command to copy the **stuff** file to a different name. Since you should at all times practice responsible file management, you'll want to use a file-name that will help you find it and other similar files more easily. A good way of doing this is to stick a descriptive suffix to the original filename. One route to go it to stick *.copy* or *.bak* (short for *backup*) at the end of every file you're creating as a backup to an existing file. In this fashion, the following command line will create a copy of the file **stuff** and store the copy under the filename **stuff.bak** in the same directory:

```
$ cp stuff stuff.bak
```

You can also use the **cp** command to copy a file to a new name in another direc-tory. If, for example, you're storing **stuff** in the directory named **data**, you may want to create a directory specifically to house file **backups**, named backups, logically enough. The following command line will create a copy of the file **stuff** and store the file under the name **stuff.bak** in the **backups** directory:

```
$ cp stuff /usr/users/yourname/backups/stuff.bak
```

If you don't specify a filename—as we did with **stuff.bak**, then the original filename will be used. For example, the following command:

```
$ cp stuff /usr/users/yourname/backups
```

will give a new file named **stuff** in the **/usr/users/yourname/backups** directo-ry. Unless you're very careful, you'll want to avoid this sort of thing—the more precise you can be with filenames, the better. Having multiple versions of the same filename scattered about your filesystem will lead you to trouble.

Finally, you can use **cp** to copy the contents of an entire directory, provided you use the *-r* option on the command line. For instance, if you want to copy the entire contents of a directory named **memos** into a new directory named **memosbackup**, you'd use the following command:

```
$ cp -r /usr/users/yourname/memos /usr/users/yourname/memosbackup
```

The Command Reference for the **cp** command, as well as other options, can be found in Table 3.1.

▼

TABLE 3.1 COMMAND REFERENCE FOR THE CP COMMAND

cp *options sourcefile destinationfile*

cp *options file1 directory*

cp *options directory1 directory2*

PURPOSE

The **cp** command copies the contents of one file into another file with a new name, or into another directory, retaining the existing filename. It also copies the content of one directory into a new directory.

OPTIONS

-i   Checks with you before overwriting existing file.

-p   Retains existing file permissions (not available on all systems).

-r   Copies entire directory.

Reality Check: Avoiding Disasters With Cp

Take Your time

The UNIX operating system assumes that you know what you're doing. Of course, if you knew what you were doing, you wouldn't be messing with a book aimed at beginners, would you?

For example: The **cp** command is pretty inflexible when it comes to protecting us from ourselves. If we use it to copy a file and a file with that very same name already exists, UNIX will go ahead and overwrite the existing file. You lose.

That's why the *-i* option is so very important. If you use it all the time—and smart UNIX users do—you can avoid overwriting files or even entire directories. The *-i* option tells the system not to overwrite an existing file; instead, the system will confirm the command and warn you that a file already exists. If you do indeed want to overwrite the existing file, you go ahead and type **y** to the query. If you don't want to overwrite the existing file, you'll type **n** and wipe your brow as you narrowly avoid what could be a disaster.

Using Mv to Move and Rename Files

If you want to move a file to a location on the directory tree, you'll use the **mv** command.

Mv, which is short for *move*, moves a file to the new location. The difference between **mv** and **cp** is that **mv** moves the file into a new location without leaving a trace of the original file, while the **cp** command creates a copy of a file in a new location while leaving the old file intact.

Using **mv** on the command line is simple:

```
$ mv oldfile newfile
```

where *oldfile* is the name of the original file, and *newfile* is the name of the file to be moved.

For example, let's say you wanted to move the file **stuff** into a directory called **archives**. In this instance, you'd need to specify both the file named **stuff** and the new destination within a command line, as follows:

```
$ mv stuff /users/you/archives
```

You can also use the **mv** command to rename files. UNIX lacks a command that specifically changes the name of files; since **mv** performs this function, there was never a need to add such a redundant feature.

For instance, to rename the file **stuff** to **mystuff** and leave it in the same directory, you'd use the following command line:

```
$ mv stuff mystuff
```

In this situation, the file named **stuff** will disappear, while a new file named **mystuff** will appear in the same directory.

You can also rename a file when moving it to another directory. In a situation where you want to rename a file from **stuff** to **mystuff** and move it to a directory named **/users/you/archives**, you'd use the following command line:

```
$ mv stuff /users/you/archives/mystuff
```

In this case, the file named **stuff** will disappear from the current directory, while a new file named **mystuff** will appear in the **/users/you/archives** directory.

Some things to remember when using the **mv** command:

▲ You don't need to specify the name of the new file in the new location when using the **mv** command to move a file to a new directory. Only specify a new filename when you actually want to change the filename.

▲ If you specify a new filename that is the same as an existing file, UNIX won't cut you any slack—it will overwrite the contents of the old file with the contents of the new file. To avoid this problem, you may want to use the **mv** command with the -i option all the time.

The -i option will confirm that you want to overwrite an existing file as a result of the **mv** command—the same as it's used with the **cp** command, which you learned about in the previous section. To use it to move the file named **stuff** to a directory named **/users/you/archives** and rename the file to **mystuff**, you'd use the following command line:

```
$ mv -i stuff /users/you/archives/mystuff
```

The filename **stuff**, as well as the rest of the filenames in this chapter, are purely arbitrary and fictitious. Go ahead and use your own filenames.

Other options are listed in Table 3.2, the Command Reference for the **mv** command.

TABLE 3.2 COMMAND REFERENCE FOR THE MV COMMAND

mv *options sources target*

PURPOSE

The **mv** command is used to move a file or a set of files to another directory or to a new filename in the current directory.

OPTIONS

-f   Moves file without checking in case you're overwriting an existing file.

-i   Checks with you before overwriting existing file.

Making Directories with Mkdir

In Chapter 2, you were repeatedly lectured about the importance of good file management, and that one of the best tools for good file management was the creation of subdirectories devoted to specific topics.

The UNIX command for creating subdirectories is **mkdir**, which is short for *make directory*, and it does only one thing: It creates a subdirectory of the current directory. Using it is easy:

```
$ mkdir dirname(s)
```

where *dirname(s)* refers to the new directory name, or multiple directory names if you prefer. For instance, to create a new directory called **newdirect**, you'd use the following command:

```
$ mkdir newdirect
```

▼

If you were doing a listing of the current directory with the **ls** command, you'd find that there was a new subdirectory called **newdirect**.

You can also use **mkdir** to create more than one sub-directory on a command line. To create subdirectories named **newdirect1** and **newdirect**2, you'd use the following command line:

```
$ mkdir newdirect1 newdirect2
```

There's not a whole lot to the **mkdir** command past the creation of new directories, as you'll see in Table 3.3, which contains the Command Reference for the command.

TABLE 3.3 COMMAND REFERENCE FOR THE MKDIR COMMAND

mkdir *option directories*

PURPOSE
The **mkdir** command creates a new directory.

OPTIONS
-m *mode*   Specifies the *mode* of the new directory.

Removing Files with Rm

If you want to give your system administrator a heart attack (or a good scare, anyway), tell him or her that you've been creating 20 or 30 files a day, but that you've not bothered to delete any of your own files. One of the biggest problems a system administrator faces is dealing with a hard disk crammed full of files and running out of disk space when users don't bother to delete old or purely redundant files. This isn't to say that you shouldn't be making backups of important files, but you shouldn't keep unneeded files on the UNIX filesystem just because it's a handy method of storage.

File cabinets are wonderful storage units, especially for information that may be needed sometime in the future but aren't needed for your daily work; examples would be old e-mail messages from far-flung friends or Christmas e-mail that you sent to everyone on your mailing list. And a file cabinet is much cheaper than a hard disk when it comes to storage.

In these situations, you'll want to use **rm** to remove files that aren't needed.

Using **rm** is about as simple as you'd expect:

```
$ rm filename(s)
```

where *filename(s)* refers to the file or files you wish to remove. You can use **rm** in many different ways. To remove a single file named **stuff** contained within the current directory, you'd use the following:

```
$ rm stuff
```

To remove files named **stuff** and **mystuff** from the current directory, you'd use the following:

```
$ rm stuff mystuff
```

You can also use the **rm** command in directories other than the current directory. For instance, to remove the file **stuff** from the **/users/you/archive**s directory, you'd use the following command line:

```
$ rm /users/you/archives/stuff
```

Wildcards, which you'll cover in Chapter 4, allow you to extend the capabilities of the **rm** command to remove multiple files with a single command. This capability becomes useful when you are clearing directories of multiple files—and especially handy if you've been practicing good file management, the kind that's been stressed repeatedly throughout this book. For example: You've been preparing annual reports for your boss since 1988, and you have been storing them with consistent filenames, beginning with **report** and ending with a suffix linked to the date of the report (**report.1988, report.1989**, and so on). Since you've been conscious of good file management, you have been storing the files in the same

▼

directory, called **reports**, along with other reports on different topics. If you were to list the contents of the **reports** directory, then, you'd see the following:

```
$ ls
notes            report.1990      report 1993      stuff
report.1988      report.1991      report.1994      to-do
report.1989      report.1992      report.bak       washington
```

Since you and your boss both have paper copies of your reports, it's clearly not essential that you keep copies of your old reports on the UNIX system. Therefore, you decide to erase all of the files that begin with **report**.

The commonality here, of course, is that the files you want to erase begin with the text string *report*. You can use a wildcard (*) to represent the rest of the filename. To erase all of the files beginning with *report* from the current directory, you'd use the following command line:

```
$ rm report*
```

If you were to run the **ls** command on the current directory, you'd see the following:

```
$ ls
notes stuff to-do washington
```

The **rm** command works on files as well as directories. Remember, a directory is nothing more than a file that contains the names of other files.

Rm is a very powerful command. If you're sloppy in its usage, you could end up erasing many files that you didn't want to erase. Many beginners, for instance, aren't as careful as they should be when using wildcards, and UNIX is certainly not as forgiving to the mistakes of beginning users as it should be. If you were to accidentally type the following command line:

```
$ rm ] *
```

you'd be in trouble, because the system would erase *every* file in the current directory without any warning to you or verification from you. And these files would be truly lost: UNIX lacks a tools for unerasing files that have been accidentally erased (by contrast, both DOS and the Macintosh operating system contain tools for bringing back files that have been erased).

You can also make subtle mistakes when using the wildcard and still get burned. For instance, if you were to accidentally type in the following command:

```
$ rm 1 *
```

instead of

```
$ rm 1*
```

you'll end up erasing *every* file in the directory, not the files beginning with *l*. Because of the potential for such mistakes, be sure to use the *-i* command when working with the **rm** command. This runs the command in *interactive* mode (the same way the *-i* option works with the **cp** and **mv** commands), and you'll be prompted to verify that you do indeed want to erase a file. To do so, you'd use a command line similar to the following:

```
$ rm -i filename(s)
```

where *filename*(s) refers to the files you want to erase.

Other options are listed in Table 3.4, the Command Reference for the **rm** command.

TABLE 3.4 COMMAND REFERENCE FOR THE RM COMMAND

rm *options file(s)*

PURPOSE

The **rm** command removes files from the UNIX system, provided you have the proper file permissions to do so. This command can be used also to delete directories (remember, a directory is merely a file containing information about other files).

OPTIONS

-f	Removes files without checking with you.
-i	Remove files only after checking with you.

▼

Removing Directories with Rmdir

The **rmdir** does to directories what **rm** does to files: It removes them.

Command

The **rmdir** command works similarly to the other commands covered in this chapter, as it works directly on a specified directory:

```
$ rmdir directory
```

where *directory* is the name of the directory you want to remove.

However, **rmdir** is designed a little differently than **rm**—with users like you in mind. If there are any files or directories within the directory you want removed, the **rmdir** command will tell you so:

```
$ rmdir llama
rmdir: llama not empty
```

In this case, you'll need to erase the contents of the **llama** directory—both files and subdirectories—before running the **rmdir** command again.

There are two options that you might use when using **rmdir**—though it's not very likely. Still, they are listed in Table 3.5, the Command Reference for the **rmdir** command.

TABLE 3.5 COMMAND REFERENCE FOR THE RMDIR COMMAND

rmdir *options directory*

PURPOSE

The **rmdir** command removes a directory, provided that it contains no files.

OPTIONS

-p   Remove *directory* and any parent directory that is empty as a result of the action.

-s   Ignore error messages.

▼

Reality Check: When Rmdir is Balky

There are times when you'll use **rmdir** on a directory you think is empty, but **rmdir** tells you otherwise. Why the disparity? Flash back to Chapter 2 and the discussion of hidden files. **Rmdir** won't remove a directory containing hidden files; hence, the balking.

To check for hidden files in a directory, use the following command:

```
$ ls -a
```

If this command returns anything other than . and .., you'll need to remove the hidden files. If you want to lob the UNIX equivalent of a grenade into the directory and make sure that *every* file is removed, use the following command:

```
$ rm .[a-zA-Z] .??
```

Searching for Information Within Files

Since you'll probably create many files and won't retain an exact memory of the contents of each file, you'll probably need more than a few tools to search through these files for specific pieces of information. UNIX features several tools for file searches, which you'll learn about in this section.

Using Find to Find a File

By far the most general tool for finding a specific file is the **find** command. Indeed, it does exactly what the name implies—it does indeed find a file.

The **find** command will find many files if you aren't very specific with your options, or it won't find the file you want if you don't provide the proper options.

These options, as listed in Table 3.6, are related to when the file was created or when it was last used. The options as listed in Table 3.6 aren't all of the available options for this flexible command, but they're the ones you are most likely to use in the course of your daily computing chores. By and large, the options listed in Table 3.6 related to when a file was created or when it was last used.

The **find** command can be demystified through a few examples. Let's say you're cleaning house and want to clear the clutter in your home directory. You know that you want to get rid of a number of older files, so you want to generate a list of older filenames and review them in order to prune the dead wood. In this case, you'll want to see a list of files that are older than 30 days. From this list you can then decide which files can go. The command line to accomplish this task would be:

```
$ find $HOME -ctime +30 -print
```

The *-ctime* option tells the system to base the search on when the file was last accessed. The *+30* option indicate that the system should look for files that were accessed more than 30 days ago. The *-print* option is mandatory, as it prints the results of the search to your screen; without it, you'll never see what files the **find** command found.

You can also base a search on the filename, either using a specific filename or wildcards, which you learned about in Chapter 2. Let's say you want to find the many backup files you've been squirreling away in your home directory. Since you've been a good UNIX user and ended the filename of each backup with a **.bak** suffix, you can imagine how easy it will be to find these many files and generate a listing. This would be accomplished using the following command line:

```
$ find $HOME -name '*.bak' -print
```

The *-name* option tells the system that we want to base the search on the name of the file. The *-name* option must be followed by a string, which is then matched to files. Since we're using wildcards, we need to use single quotation marks (') to surround the string of text. And, as with the previous search, the *-print* option prints the results of the search to your screen; without it, you'll never see what files the **find** command found.

Other important options to the **find** command are listed in Table 3.6, the Command Reference for the **find** command.

TABLE 3.6 COMMAND REFERENCE FOR THE FIND COMMAND

find *pathname(s) condition(s)*

PURPOSE

The **find** command, in essence, finds a file, based on the criteria you provide with a slew of options.

OPTIONS

-atime *days*	Finds files that were accessed:
	+d more than *d* days ago
	d exactly *d* days ago
	-d fewer than *d* days ago
-ctime *days*	Finds files that were changed:
	+d more than *d* days ago
	d exactly *d* days ago
	-d fewer than *d* days ago
-local	Search for files on the local filesystem
-mtime *days*	Finds files that were modified:
	+d more than *d* days ago
	d exactly *d* days ago
	-d fewer than *d* days ago
-name *file*	Finds a file named *file*.
-newer *filename*	Returns all files that have been modified more recently than *filename*.
-print	Prints the results of the search to the screen. This option is mandatory, if you want to see the results of your search.
-type *t*	Returns names of files of type *t*. Type *t* can be **b** (block special file), **c** (character special file), **d** (directory), **f** (plain file), **l** (symbolic link), or **p** (pipe).
-user *user*	Matches files belonging to a user, specified by name or ID.

▼

Searching with Grep

The **grep** command looks through a file or set of files in search of a specific text string.

The **grep** command involves only the string to find and the files to search:

```
$ grep string file(s)
```

where *string* is the desired text string and *file(s)* refers to the file or files to search. **grep** will then return the line in the specified file containing the string.

The best way to learn about the **grep** command is to see how it's used in a variety of situations. For instance, you may want to search a specific file for a specific string. The corresponding command line would be like this:

```
$ grep profits report.1994
The profits for the project far outweighed
```

Grep can also be used to look for more than one word. In this case, you'll need to enclose the words with quotation marks, or else the system will assume that the second word is a command of some sort. The resulting command line would look like:

```
$ grep "profits for" report.1994
The profits for the project far outweighed
```

As always, wildcards can be used in a UNIX command. Particularly useful is the use of a wildcard in lieu of a filename, since the typical search for a string isn't limited to a single file. To search through all of the files in a directory for a string, simply use a wildcard (*) instead of specifying a file"

```
$ grep "profits for" *
report.1993: The profits for this year are down,
report.1994: The profits for the project far outweighed
```

You could also use a wildcard within the text to search for. If, for example, you don't recall the name of a person you sent a memo to in 1993, but you remember that the person's last name began with *Di*, you could use the two characters in conjunction with a wildcard, as follows:

```
$ grep "Di*" *
memo.211993: To: Tommy DiGregorio
```

```
note.331992: Dire consequences will follow if
warning.note: Digging in forbidden areas will
```

Some rules for working with **grep**:

▲ **Grep** is an amazingly literal command. If you're looking for the word *profit* in a file, **grep** will return a line containing *profits*, *profitable*, *unprofitable*, or *profit*. In other words, **grep** doesn't look for the word *profit*, but rather the six specific letters, all in a row.

▲ As with everything else in UNIX, case counts when using the **grep** command. If you use a command line that uses **grep** to look for the string *profits for*, but the instance you're looking for actually begins a sentence, **grep** will not report a match, since *profits for* is different than *Profits for*. If you're not quite sure of the case of the string you're looking for, you can use the *-i* option, which tells **grep** to ignore the case of the string:

```
$ grep -i "profits for" *
report.1994: The profits for this year are down,
report.1993: The profits for the project far outweighed
notes.1994: Profits for 1994 were up more than 15
```

Other options are listed in Table 3.7.

▲ **Grep** sticks to one line at a time. If you searched for the string *profits for*, and the file was formatted in such a way where *profits* ended one line and *for* began the next, **grep** will not report a match.

▲ If you merely want to verify the existence of a string within a file, but you don't want to see the line containing the string, use the *-l* option:

```
$ grep -l "profits for" *
report.1994
report.1993
```

▲ **Grep** can be used on its own, but it becomes especially useful when used in conjunction with other commands. For example, you may want to identify all of the commands in your current directory that were created by a co-worker named Greg. Remember that a pipe can be used to send the output of one file to be used as input for another command. To find out which files Greg created, you could either list all of the files in your directory with the **ls** command and scan through the resulting listing, hoping to note the filenames before they scroll by. The alternative is to pipe the results of the **ls** command, either to a file or directly to **grep**. The easiest thing to do, of

▼

course, is just pipe the information created by **ls** to **grep**. Since you want to know who owns the file, you'll use the *-l* option to **ls**:

```
$ ls -l | grep "greg"
-rw-rw-rw- 1 greg group1 Feb 2 09:20 ltimer
-rw-rw-rw- 1 greg group1 Nov 19 21:20 data
$
```

▲ The *-v* option turns **grep** into the anti-**grep**, returning files and lines that *don't* contain the specified string. This probably isn't an option you'll use often, but when you need it, it's there.

Other options are listed in Table 3.7.

TABLE 3.7 COMMAND REFERENCE FOR THE GREP COMMAND

grep *options pattern file(s)*

PURPOSE

The **grep** command searches for text in a file or multiple files, and then it displays the results of the search.

OPTIONS

-c	Returns the number of matches, without quoting the text.
-h	Returns matched text with no reference to filenames.
-i	Ignores the case of the string to search for.
-l	Returns filenames containing a match, without quoting the text.
-n	Returns line number of matched text, as well as the text itself.
-v	Returns lines that do *not* match the text.

Egrep and Fgrep: Kissing Cousins

Two "improvements" to the basic **grep** command are **fgrep** and **egrep**. If you're using a newer UNIX system, you'll be able to use these commands, but if you're using an older UNIX system, they may not be supported on your system.

▼

Both **fgrep** and **egrep** do everything that **grep** does, but they add one handy feature: They will search for multiple strings within the same command line. For instance, you can search for all the memos you sent to both Jan and Greg—but not necessarily to both. To search for both *Jan* and *Greg* with **egrep**, you need to enclose both within quotations marks, separated by the pipe symbol. Here's an example of a typical **egrep** command line that will search for both *Jan* and *Greg*:

```
$ egrep "Jan|Greg" *
brady.1994: Dear Jan:
brady.1993: Dear Greg:
```

The command reference for **egrep** is listed in Table 3.8.

TABLE 3.8 COMMAND REFERENCE FOR THE EGREP COMMAND

egrep *options text file(s)*

PURPOSE

Searches for text in a file or multiple files, displaying the results of the search.

OPTIONS

-c	Returns the number of matches, without quoting the text.
-e *string*	Used to search for *string* beginning with a hyphen (-).
-f *file*	Takes text from file *file*.
-h	Returns only matched text with no reference to filenames.
-i	Ignores the case of the text.
-l	Returns only filenames containing a match, without quoting the text.
-n	Returns line number of matched text, as well as the text itself.
-v	Returns lines that do *not* match the text.

To search for both *Jan* and *Greg* with **fgrep** (which is short for *fast grep*, by the way), each string must be placed on its own line within the command line:

```
$ fgrep "Jan
Greg" *
brady.1994: Dear Jan:
brady.1993: Dear Greg:
```

The options for the **fgrep** command are listed in Table 3.9.

TABLE 3.9 COMMAND REFERENCE FOR THE FGREP COMMAND

fgrep *options text file(s)*

PURPOSE

Searches for text in a file or multiple files, displaying the results of the search. However, **fgrep** searches only for literal text strings. It will not search for expressions.

OPTIONS

-b	Returns block number of matched line.
-c	Returns only the number of matches, without quoting the text.
-e *string*	Used to search for *strings* beginning with a hyphen (-).
-f *file*	Takes the text string from file *file*.
-h	Returns only matched text with no reference to filenames.
-i	Ignores the case of the text to search for.
-l	Returns filenames containing a match, without quoting the text.
-n	Returns line number of matched text, as well as the text itself.
-v	Returns lines that do *not* match the text.
-x	Returns a line only of the *string* matches an entire line.

▼

Reality Check: Fgrep

In theory, this is how **fgrep** should work. However, on many systems, the **fgrep** is merely a gussied-up version of the **grep** command, running a little faster, but not supporting all options traditionally supported by **grep**. The faux **fgrep** also does not support searches for multiple strings. Check your system documentation to see exactly what your **fgrep** will do.

Sorting The Contents of Files

UNIX tends to be a fussy operating system. When it comes to organizing data, UNIX loves to have things just so, which you'll find as you use some of the more advanced UNIX commands. That's why there are several commands that can be used to organize the contents of files. Chief among these commands in the **sort** command.

Again, the easiest way to learn how the **sort** command works is to see it in action. As a frivolous example: You're a baseball fan, and you've entered the teams in the American League Central in a file called **AL_Central**. You've not really paid much attention to the order when you created the file, so the file looks something like this (as seen with the **cat** command)

```
$ cat AL_Central
Minnesota
Milwaukee
Chicago
Cleveland
Kansas City
```

If you are from Chicago, you don't like the fact that *Minnesota* leads off the file, so you decide to put *Chicago* in its rightful alphabetical spot on the top of the file. The **sort** command changes the alphabetical order of lines within a file, so you decide to use it on your **AL_Central** file:

```
$ sort AL_Central
Chicago
Cleveland
```

▼

```
Kansas City
Milwaukee
Minnesota
```

However, your original file will remain unchanged, as the **sort** command writes its standard output to the screen, not to a file or a printer. If you wanted your **AL_Central** file to reflect changes made by the **sort** command, you'll have to redirect the output to a file, as you learned about in Chapter 2.

To direct the results of the **sort** command to a new file named **AL_Cen.sort**, you'd use the following command line:

```
$ sort AL_Central > AL_Cen.sort
$
```

Because you've redirected the results of the **sort** command to a file, nothing appears on the screen. However, if you were to view the contents of the new file named **AL_Cen.sort**, you'd see the following:

```
$ cat AL_Cen.sort
Chicago
Cleveland
Kansas City
Milwaukee
Minnesota
```

If you were to try and write the results of the **sort** command to the same file-name, the system would generate an error message. This safeguard exists so that beginning users like yourself don't accidentally sort a file and make the changes permanent. (In fact, it's a good idea to *always* view the results of a sort on the screen before committing them to a file.) However, obviously there are times when you do want to overwrite an existing file. In this situation, you're not using the UNIX redirection procedure, but rather an option associated with the **sort** command, -o:

```
$ sort -o AL_Central AL_Central
```

The use of the *sort* suffix here is purely arbitrary and not the direct result of using the **sort** command. However, when you're keeping track of many files, a good way to tell them apart is to place a distinctive suffix onto files, especially one linked to the steps used to create them. This practice will be used throughout this chapter.

▲ **L E A R N   M O R E   A B O U T** ▲

If you're still a little fuzzy about standard input/output and redirection, a review of Chapter 2 is definitely in order.

Other options are listed in Table 3.10.

TABLE 3.10 COMMAND REFERENCE FOR THE SORT COMMAND

sort *options files*

PURPOSE

The **sort** command sorts the lines of files, usually in alphabetical order. Commands like **comm** and **join** require sorted files in order to work, which is the real reason for the existence of **sort**—not to arrange baseball standings.

OPTIONS

-b	Ignores leading spaces and tabs.
-c	Checks if *files* are already sorted. If they are, **sort** does nothing.
-d	Sorts in dictionary order (ignore punctuation).
-f	Ignores the case of the sort entries.
-i	Ignores non-ASCII characters when sorting.
-m	Merges files that have already been sorted.
-M	Sorts the files assuming the first three characters are months.
-n	Sorts in numeric order.
-ofile	Stores output in *file*. The default is to send output to standard output.
-r	Reverses the order of the sort—starting either with the end of the alphabet or the largest numeral.
-zn	Provides a maximum of *n* characters per line of input.
+n[-m]	Skips *n* fields before sorting, and then sorts through line *m*.

Command

The **sort** command can be used to sort multiple files. To combine and alphabetize the entire American League, you'd use the following:

```
$ sort AL_West AL_Central AL_East
Baltimore
Boston
California
Chicago
Cleveland
Detroit
Kansas City
Milwaukee
Minnesota
New York
Oakland
Seattle
Texas
Toronto
$
```

Redirection also can be used with multiple files:

```
$ sort AL_West AL_Central AL_East > American
$
```

Not every sort you need is going to be alphabetical, however—many will be numerical in nature. For instance, if you're maintaining the standings of the American League Central (complete with wins and losses), you'll want to do sorts on a numerical basis, not alphabetical. To sort a file by numeral, use the *-n* options:

```
$ sort -n AL_Central
```

Here's what the resulting file would look like after such a sort:

```
$ sort -n AL_Central
10 50 Milwaukee
20 40 Kansas City
30 30 Cleveland

40 20 Chicago
49 11 Minnesota
```

The three columns seen above are referred to as *fields* in UNIX parlance. For the **sort** command to work, each of the lines must be consistent in the number of fields within the lines, and also in the organization of the fields.

For what we want to do, the *-n* option takes us only part of the way. In this situation, we want to sort the files in reverse order, showing that the team with the most wins is at the top of the standings. In this case, you'd want to use the *-r* options in conjunction with the *-n* option:

```
$ sort -rn AL_Central
49 11 Minnesota
40 20 Chicago
30 30 Cleveland
20 40 Kansas City
10 50 Milwaukee
```

The **sort** command can also be used to sort based on a specific column, not necessarily the beginning of the line, as shown in the following two examples:

```
$ sort +1 AL_Central
49 11 Minnesota
40 20 Chicago
30 30 Cleveland
20 40 Kansas City
10 50 Milwaukee

$ sort +2 AL_Central
40 20 Chicago
30 30 Cleveland
20 40 Kansas City
10 50 Milwaukee
49 11 Minnesota
```

There's no limit to the number of columns you can skip when using the *+n* option (where *n* refers to the number of columns to be skipped).

Reality Check: Using Sort

For some reason or another, beginners tend to have a tough time with the **sort** command. Often they'll use **sort** and find that the data returned by **sort** isn't what they expected.

▼

There's one simple reason for this: They are using **sort** on a file that isn't formatted consistently. When using the *-r* and *-n* options, for instance, beginners will throw in a few lines that don't begin with numerals. Or, when using the *+n* option, they'll have three columns in one line, four in another, and two in a third line—but then they expect **sort** to know which column to sort.

UNIX is a fussy and precise operating system. It will do *exactly* as you tell it. And since there's often not a lot of interaction associated with UNIX commands, you need to make sure that all elements of the command line are precise.

File Comparisons With Comm and Cmp

UNIX also includes several tools for comparing files.

One of the most commonly used tool is **comm**, which is used to compare sorted files. Why sorted files? Because **comm** does line-by-line comparisons. If the files aren't similar in order and structure, the results of the **comm** command aren't going to mean much.

However, there's one huge drawback to the **comm** command: It works only on text files—and sorted text files, to boot. It won't work with any program files, nor will it work with any specially formatted files that are created by applications like *AutoCAD* or *FrameMaker*.

Keeping with the baseball motif: Let's say you wanted to compare the contents of the **American** file with the contents of the **National** file. You've already sorted both files, so the entries are in alphabetical order. The resulting command line and output would look like this:

```
$ comm American National
              Atlanta
```

▼

```
Baltimore
Boston
California
                                            Chicago
                    Cincinnati
Cleveland
                    Colorado
Detroit
                    Florida
                    Houston
Kansas City
                    Los Angeles
Milwaukee
Minnesota
                    Montreal
                                            New York
Oakland
                    Philadelphia
                    Pittsburgh
                    San Diego
                    San Francisco
Seattle
                    St. Louis
Texas
Toronto
```

The output is organized in three columns: Column 1 lists lines unique to the first file listed on the command line (in this case, **American**), Column 2 lists lines unique to the second file listed on the command line (in this case, **National**), and Column 3 lists lines occurring in both files.

Like all UNIX commands, you can save the results of the **comm** command into a file using redirection. In this case, you're saving the results of the above **comm** command into a file called **baseball.sort:**

```
$ comm American National > baseball.sort
```

Perhaps more useful in most situations (though not this specific example) is the -u option to **comm**, which compares two files and eliminates redundancies:

```
$ comm -u American National > baseball.comm
```

▼

▼

This command saves the comparison done by **comm** to the file **baseball.comm**, with only one *Chicago* line and one *New York* line.

Other options to the **comm** command are listed in Table 3.11.

The *-u* option isn't supported on some older UNIX systems, though it is included in System V Release 4.

TABLE 3.11 COMMAND REFERENCE FOR THE COMM COMMAND

comm *options file1 file2*

PURPOSE

The **comm** command compares the contents of two presorted text files. The output is generated in three columns:

Lines found in file1	Lines found in file2	Lines found in both files

OPTIONS

-1	Suppresses the printing of column 1.
-2	Suppresses the printing of column 2.
-3	Suppresses the printing of column 3.
-12	Prints only column 3.
-13	Prints only column 2.
-23	Prints only column 1.

Of course, there are other commands used to compare files.

▼

One of the simplest such commands is the **cmp** command, which tells you if two files are different; if they are, **cmp** prints out the first line that is different in the two files. Again, this command helps you to better manage the multitude of files that you'll create throughout your normal work.

After looking through two files with the **cat** command, you'll see how the **cmp** command works:

```
$ cat brady.1993
Dear Brady:
It's time for another hokey television
reunion! As you know, this year's theme
is to be how Marcia has dealt with
the loss of a loved one. I'm sure you'll
agree that we have another hit on our
hands! I look forward to seeing you on
March 12, 1993.
--Your producer

$ cat brady.1994
Dear Brady:

It's time for another hokey television
reunion! As you know, this year's theme
is to be how Greg has dealt with
the loss of a loved one. I'm sure you'll
agree that we have another hit on our
hands! I look forward to seeing you on
April 16, 1994.
--Your producer

$ cmp brady.1993 brady.1994
brady.1993 brady.1994 differ: char 14, line 4
```

The **cmp** command reports that the first difference between **brady.1993** and **brady.1994** occurs in the fourth line, in the 14th character. This is *all* the **cmp** command will tell you—you won't know to what extent the files differ, nor will you know other specific instances where the files differ.

There are a few options of dubious worth, as listed in Table 3.12.

TABLE 3.12 COMMAND REFERENCE FOR THE CMP COMMAND

cmp *options file1 file2*

PURPOSE

The **cmp** command compares the contents of two files. If the files are different, **cmp** returns the byte position and line number of the first difference between the two files. If there is no difference in the files, then **cmp** returns nothing. The **cmp** command works on all files, not just text files. Similar commands, such as **diff** and **comm**, work only with text files.

OPTIONS

-l   Displays the byte position and the differing characters for all differences within the file.

-s   Works silently, returning only the exit codes and not the instances of differences. The exit code is one of the following:

    0   Files are identical.

    1   Files are different.

    2   One of the files is unreadable.

Using Diff to Discover More Information

For more extensive information, you'll want to use the **diff** command.

The **diff** command first reports if the files are different, and then lists each instance where the files differ. Using the two files above as examples, you can see how **diff** works:

```
$ diff brady.1993 brady.1994
4c4
< is to be how Marcia has dealt with
- - -
```

```
> is to be how Greg has dealt with
8c8
< March 12, 1993.
- - -
> April 16, 1994.
```

Even on short files with only nine lines, **diff** reports a lot of information. Lines beginning with the < symbol occur in the first file listed on the command line, while lines beginning with the > symbol occur within the second file listed on the command line. The dashed line separates the two lines. The numerals refer to the specific lines that differ.

The Command Reference for the **diff** command can be found in Table 3.13.

TABLE 3.13 COMMAND REFERENCE FOR THE DIFF COMMAND

diff *options diroptions file1 file2*

PURPOSE

The **diff** command compares two files and reports differing lines. The line numbers of the differing lines are noted, while the unique line from *file1* is marked with <, and the unique line from *file2* is marked with >. Three hyphens (—-) separate the contents of the two files. This command works best with text files.

OPTIONS

-b   Ignores blanks at the end of line.

-i   Ignores case.

-t   Expands tabs in output to spaces.

-w   Ignores spaces and tabs.

▼

There are many variations on **diff** within the various versions of UNIX, each slightly different than the main **diff** command.

Bdiff, for example, works best with long files, while the **diff3** is used to compare three files. And the ever-popular **sdiff** command reports which lines are the same and which are different.

The Command Reference for **bdiff** can be found in Table 3.14; the Command Reference for **diff3** can be found in Table 3.15.

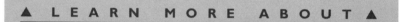

▲ L E A R N   M O R E   A B O U T ▲

As you'll see by the options listed in Table 3.15, it works best as a front end for a text editor named **ed**, which you'll learn about in Chapter 6.

The Command Reference for **sdiff** can be found in Table 3.16.

TABLE 3.14 COMMAND REFERENCE FOR THE BDIFF COMMAND

bdiff *file1 file2 options*

PURPOSE

The **bdiff** command compares two files and reports on the differing lines. This command invokes the **diff** command after dividing a file into manageable chunks—thus making it more suitable than **diff** when it comes to larger files—and it works best with text files.

OPTIONS

-n   Divides the files into segments *n* lines long.

-s   Suppresses error messages.

TABLE 3.15 COMMAND REFERENCE FOR THE DIFF3 COMMAND

diff3 options file1 file2 file3

PURPOSE

The **diff3** command compares three different files and reports the differences. Returns one of the following codes:

====	All three files differ.
====1	*file1* is different.
====2	*file2* is different.
====3	*file3* is different.

OPTIONS

-e   Creates an **ed** script that places differences between *file2* and *file3* into *file1*. Not available on all systems.

-E   Creates an **ed** script that places differences between *file2* and *file3* into *file1*, marking lines that differ in all three files with brackets.

-x   Creates an **ed** script that places differences between all three files.

-X   Creates an **ed** script that places differences between all three files, marking lines that differ in all three files with brackets. Not available on all systems.

-3   Creates an **ed** script that places differences between *file1* and *file3* into *file1*.

TABLE 3.16 COMMAND REFERENCE FOR THE SDIFF COMMAND

sdiff *options file1 file2*

PURPOSE

The **sdiff** command compares *file1* with *file2* and reports on the differences, as well as identical lines. Output occurs in four forms:

▼

TABLE 3.16 CONTINUED

text text	lines are identical
text <	line exists only in *file1*
text >	line exists only in *file2*
*text	text*	lines are different
OPTIONS	
-l	Report only on lines that are identical in *file1*.
-o *file*	Send identical lines to *file*.
-s	Do not return identical lines.

Using Cut to Create Lists

Throughout this section you've been told repeatedly about the importance of consistency when it comes to many UNIX commands and the files they are designed to work upon. Nowhere will this be made more clear than when you're working with the **cut** command.

If you're working with lists, you'll find that the **cut** command is very handy. It allows you to create rudimentary databases without a separate database-management system. (Indeed, on most levels, UNIX as a whole can be viewed as a rudimentary database-management system.) You can create a list of employees, for instance, and pluck out the portions of the list as you need them. You can organize a list of customers and use it to create a mailing list. Data organized in a logical, tabular form can be easily manipulated by various UNIX commands—chief among them is the **cut** command.

For **cut** to work, however, the fields within the file in question must be consistent. A *column* is exactly what the name describes—a row of characters with the same position on a line—while *fields* are separated by tabs. Both are referred to by numerals relative to the first column or field on the line. The data in one field must correspond to the fields in other lines. Many database-management packages work with fields, and UNIX file-management commands are particularly strong when it comes to working with files that have common fields (as you'll see during a later discussion of the **join** command).

Let's return to our baseball example: You can use the **cut** command to pull information out of your running standings of the American League Central—as shown by the following examples. First, let's take a look once again at the **AL_Central** file after you have finished sorting it to reflect the standings:

```
$ cat AL_Central
49 11 Minnesota

40 20 Chicago
30 30 Cleveland
20 40 Kansas City
10 50 Milwaukee
```

Let's say that you want to create a list that contains only the numbers of victories each team has. In this case, you'd use the **cut** command to grab the first and third fields of the **AL_Central** file, as accomplished by the following command line:

```
$ cut f1,3 AL_Central
49 Minnesota
40 Chicago
30 Cleveland
20 Kansas City
10 Milwaukee
```

This tells the system to cut the first and third fields of the **AL_Central** file. As with most UNIX commands, the **cut** command sends its output to the screen, not to a file or a printer. To send the results of this command to a file, you'd use the standard UNIX redirection:

```
$ cut f1,3 AL_Central > winners.cut
$ cat winners.cut
49 Minnesota
40 Chicago
30 Cleveland
20 Kansas City
10 Milwaukee
```

There is a lot of flexibility associated with the **cut** command. You could use it to grab data from more than one file, so long as the files were structured the same. For instance, to create a composite standings of the entire American League based only on wins, you could grab fields 1 and 3 from all three baseball files and then sort the files in numerical order, as shown in this command line:

```
$ cut f1,3 AL_West AL_Central AL_East | sort -rn > standings
```

Why do you need the **sort** command? Because **cut** will grab information in the order presented in the original files. If you grab information from three files, the **cut** command will list the data grabbed from the first file, followed by the data grabbed from the second file, and then the data grabbed from the third file. If you want to truly integrate the information into some order—alphabetical or numerical—you'll need to use the **sort** command to impose order onto chaotic information.

There are several options associated with the **cut** command, the most important of which are listed in Table 3.17.

TABLE 3.17 COMMAND REFERENCE FOR THE CUT COMMAND

cut *options files*

PURPOSE

The **cut** command cuts a list of columns (specified with the **-c** option) or fields (specified with the **-f** option) from a file or a set of files.

OPTIONS

-c_list_	Cuts columns specified by *list* from a file.
-d_character_	Substitutes *character* for the delimiter when the **-f** option is used. If a nonalphabetic character is to be used as the delimiter (such as a space), it must be enclosed in single quote marks.
-f_list_	Cuts fields specified by *list* from a file.

Merging Files with Paste and Join

Tearing things apart, of course, is a lot more fun than putting them together. There are two UNIX command that are frequently used to combine files: **paste** and **join**.

Essentially, the **paste** command merges two files together—*literally* side by side. The first line of the first file will be immediately followed by the first line of the second file. If you're combining files containing memos, the **paste** command won't really help, because this mashing together of lines will yield a lot of inchoate text. Instead, the **paste** command is best used when you work with files containing data in columnar or tabular form. For instance, the first two columns of the desired document may be contained in the file named **file1**, and the last two columns of the desired document may be contained in the file named **file2**. To combine the two files into a file named **file3**, you'd use the following command line:

```
$ paste file1 file2 > file3
```

There are many options associated with the **paste** command—as shown in Table 3.18, which contains the **paste** Command Reference—but perhaps the handiest options is the *-d* option, which allows you to specify a character used to separate the fields (the default is a tab). For instance, a common format for database-management packages is *comma delimited*, where commas, and not spaces or tabs, are used to separate the fields of a file. By using the *-d* option, as shown in the following command line, you can specify the comma, instead of the default tab, to be used as a delimiter:

```
$ paste -d',' file1 file2 > file 3
```

One thing to remember when using the **paste** command: Unless you specify a file that contains the merged data, the results of the command will be printed only to the screen.

Other options, as well as variances within the *-d* option, are listed in Table 3.18.

TABLE 3.18 COMMAND REFERENCE FOR THE PASTE COMMAND

paste *options file(s)*

PURPOSE

The **paste** command merges files and places the corresponding lines side by side. For instance, the first line of *file1* will be followed by the first line of *file2* in a second column; a tab separates the two columns.

OPTIONS

-            Use standard input as input for the command.

d'*char***'**   Uses *char* as the delimiter between columns, instead of the default tab. *Char* can be any character, or one of the following:

     \n   newline

     \t   tab

     ****   backslash

For most tasks, however, you'll want to use the **join** command to combine files.

The **join** command combines files that contain a common field. For example, you may be working with several different files that contain information regarding your company's employees. One file, **extensions**, may list the name of the employee, followed by an extension; another file, **netnames**, may list the network names of the employees in a similar fashion—the name of the employee, followed by the network name. Because this information can just as easily be kept in a single file, you decide to join the two files. You've already sorted the two files with the **sort** command, ensuring that the names of the employees are in the same order in both files—a situation that can be confirmed by using the **cat** command to view the contents of both files:

```
$ cat extensions
Chris 29
Kevin 24
Natasha 26
Sean  21

$ cat netnames
Chris spike
Kevin kevin
Natasha natasha
Sean   sean
```

As you can see, the two files have a common field—the first field, which lists the names of the employees. To join the two files into one larger file, you'd use the following command line:

```
$ join extension netnames > names
```

Again, remember to redirect the output of this command, or the results of the command will be printed only to the screen, and not to a file.

To view the new **names** file, you'd again use the **cat** command:

```
$ cat names
Chris 29 spike
Kevin 24 kevin
Natasha 26 natasha

Sean  21 sean
```

In this example, two files were joined using the first field as the key. There are times when you may want to join two files, and the common field is the first field in the first file, but it is a different field in another file. You can tell **join** to key the merger to different fields within the two files, as long as you list the specific field within the file. Continuing with our example: Let's say that you want to use the **names** file created above and combine it with another file, **locations**, which contains office numbers—only the file is organized with office numbers in the first field, followed by the employee name. (Since you're a fast-learning UNIX worker, you already know that you can sort a file with the **sort** command based on any field within a file.) The resulting sorted file looks like this:

```
$ cat locations
3161 Chris
3224 Kevin
```

▼

```
2990 Natasha
3001 Sean
```

In this instance, you'll want to join the two files based on the common field— the first field in the **names** file and the second field in the **locations** file. The following command line does just that:

```
$ join -j1 1 -j2 2 names locations > employees
```

Admittedly, the syntax of this command line is rather confusing. The *-j1 1* portion tells **join** to use the first field of the first file. The *-j2 2* portion tells **join** to use the second field of the second file. The files are specified *after* the command and options.

The resulting file will look like this:

```
$ cat employees
Chris     29     spike      3161
Kevin     24     kevin      3224
Natasha   26     natasha    2990
Sean      21     sean       3001
```

Other options are listed in Table 3.19, the Command Reference for the **join** command.

TABLE 3.19 COMMAND REFERENCE FOR THE JOIN COMMAND

join *options file1 file2*

PURPOSE

The **join** command combines two presorted files that have a common key field. Only lines containing the key field will be joined.

OPTIONS

-a*filename*	Lists lines in *filename* that cannot be joined. If *filename* is now specified, unjoinable lines from both files will be listed.
-e *string*	Replaces empty fields in output with *string*.
-j*filename m*	Joins on the *m*th field of file *filename* (or both if *filename* is not specified).
-t*char*	*char* will be used as a field separator, instead of the default.

▼

Joining Files with the Cat Command

In Chapters 1 and 2 you were exposed to the **cat** command as a method for viewing files. However, **cat**'s original purpose was to combine files— a purpose that you can use.

Using the **cat** command with files can be a little tricky, so be careful. It's easiest to learn the **cat** command by seeing how it works in various situations. For starters: You can use **cat** to create a new file that has the contents of an existing file. You must specify both the original and new file on the command line, separated by a > symbol. The command line for saving the contents of the file **thea** into a new file named **geisha** would look like this:

```
$ cat thea > geisha
```

The file **thea** would be unchanged.

You can also use **cat** to combine files. Let's say you wanted to combine the files **thea** and **geisha** into a new file named **spike**. The following command line does just that:

```
$ cat thea geisha > spike
```

The order of the files of the command line determines the content of the new file. In this instance, the contents of the file **thea** would be followed by the contents of the file **geisha**. Again, the contents of the files **thea** and **geisha** would be unchanged.

You can also use **cat** as a rudimentary text editor. If you want to open a file named **cats** and then type in its contents, you'd use the following command line:

```
$ cat > cats
```

All subsequent keyboard input would be stored in the new file named **cats**. When you're done typing into this new file, there are a few things you'll need to note:

▲ You must press the Enter key at the end of every line. If you don't, cat will refuse to accept more keystrokes.

▲ You can make changes with the Backspace key, moving back as you type. However, you can't perform any other movements via the scroll keys.

▲ When you're finished typing into the file, type Ctrl-D to end input.

Finally, you can use **cat** to append data to an existing file. The following command line places the contents of the file **thea** into an existing file named **spike**:

```
$ cat thea >> spike
```

If you want to add to a file (in this case, a file named **geisha**) directly from your keyboard, you can do so with the following command line:

```
$ cat - >> geisha
```

 If you're not careful about how you use the **cat** command, you could easily overwrite the contents of one file with keyboard entry or the contents of another file. For instance, the command:

```
$ cat - > spike
```

replaces the current contents of the file **spike** with keyboard input. **Cat** will not warn you when you're making changes to existing files, so you need to be *very* careful when using this command.

This Chapter in Review

▲ UNIX contains a number of tools used to work directly with files—either file locations or the actual contents of a files. This chapter covers the major UNIX file tools. However, there are many more file tools supported by the UNIX operating system, and chances are good that if you want to perform some obscure task, there's a UNIX command waiting for you.

▲ The **cp** command is used to copy files either to a new filename or to the same filename in a different location on the directory tree.

▲ The **mv** command is used to move an existing file elsewhere on the UNIX filesystem. It can also be used to rename files— essentially by moving them to a different name in the same or a different directory.

▲ The **mkdir** command is used to create directories.

▲ The **rm** command is used to remove files. If you're not careful, the **rm** command can do some serious damage to your filesystem, so use it with caution.

▲ There are many commands that return the differences between files: **diff**, **bdiff**, **diff3**, and **sdiff**.

▲ The **cut** command allows you to grab data from a file. However, you need to give the command very specific instructions about which data to cut.

▲ Two commands are very convenient when combining files: the **paste** and the **join** commands. However, they work only under very specific circumstances, so you'll need to apply a little elbow grease before using them.

▪ CHAPTER FOUR ▪

Learning About Your Environment and the Shell

The shell is a program that acts as an interpreter between you and the actual workings of the UNIX operating system. As such, the shell is extremely important in most day-to-day computing. This chapter explains how shells work and some features that you'll find useful. Topics include:

▲ The different shells: C shell, Bourne shell, and Korn shell.
▲ Changing your shell.
▲ Finding what shells are available on your system.
▲ Shell prompts and how to change them.
▲ Widening the search with wildcards.
▲ Mastering shell variables in your daily work.
▲ Setting your own variables.
▲ Tackling the difficult concept of standard I/O and redirection.
▲ Using pipes.
▲ Choosing a username.
▲ Passwords and how to change them.

▼

The Shell and Your Environment

As you can tell from the perhaps imposing lengths of Chapters 1, 2, and 3, learning the basics of the UNIX operating system is quite an involved task. So far, your learning has centered on how to accomplish specific tasks with UNIX. With this chapter, however, the focus shifts slightly, as you learn both how to accomplish specific tasks with UNIX and how UNIX carries out these tasks.

For starters: When you type a command into the UNIX system (as you did with the **ls** command in Chapter 2), you're not exactly communicating directly with the UNIX system. Rather, you're communicating with a program called the *shell*, which is a program specially designed to act as a buffer between you and the UNIX system. There are many different shells available, including (but not limited to):

- ▲ C shell (**csh**)
- ▲ Korn shell (**ksh**)
- ▲ Bourne shell (**sh**)
- ▲ Windowing Korn shell (**wksh**)
- ▲ Public-domain Korn shell (**pdksh**)

The shell is responsible for taking the commands you enter in the computer and translating them into a form the computer can understand. The shell also encompasses a programming language that you can use to customize your environment.

Don't worry—you won't have to tackle programming in the course of this book. But there are a few things you can do that will make your daily UNIX usage go smoother and which might be considered programming on a very rudimentary level.

The shell also determines your *environment*: information that determines your daily usage and system configuration. This chapter

▼

covers shells in general, as well as how you can use tools to automate some basic computing chores under UNIX.

Shell Games

Almost every UNIX system comes with a variety of shells. While you'll probably stick with the shell already set up for your use—at least in the initial stages of your UNIX usage—it's good to know your options.

UNIX is rather unique in that it separates the shell from the underlying operating system. DOS, for instance, includes a file called **COMMAND.COM** that is the functional equivalent of the UNIX shell. However, DOS users are stuck with the **COMMAND.COM** file that ships with their version of DOS.

The most popular shell is the oldest major shell: the Bourne shell, named after its creator, Stephen Bourne. The Bourne shell (with the filename **sh**) is pretty much the same as when Bourne introduced it in 1979.

The first real competitor to the Bourne shell came from Bill Joy (a founder of Sun Microsystems, Inc.) while he was a student at the University of California at Berkeley. His alternative, the C shell (with the filename **csh**), is also very popular these days. In many ways, the C shell resembles the popular C programming language that is the foundation of the UNIX operating system. It also contains a few neat features, such as job history and aliases, that were not found in the Bourne shell. Though this chapter focuses on shell usage in general, C shell commands and procedures will be outlined when they differ from Korn or Bourne shell commands and procedures.

The last of the Big Three shells is the Korn shell (with the filename **ksh**), written by David Korn of Bell Laboratories. The Korn shell was designed as a direct extension to the Bourne shell, which means that scripts and programs written for the Bourne shell can be used under the Korn shell without modifications. (By contrast, the C shell uses different commands than do the Bourne and Korn shells.) In addition, the Korn shell also implemented many popular features, such as job history and aliases, which had been introduced in the Bourne shell.

▼

Things like job history and aliases will be more important when you become a more experienced user. For now, they are not important to your daily computing chores.

Shells on Your System

As mentioned earlier, you'll probably want to stick with the shell already set up for your use. Although you may benefit from some of the advanced features of the Korn and C shells further in your UNIX usage, your initial shell needs will be so basic that the shell you use won't really matter. If you're curious about which shell is installed in your system, use the following command line:

```
$ echo $SHELL
```

The response will be **sh**, **csh**, **ksh**, or some other name ending in *sh*. If you want to use a different shell, you must first see what shells are available in your system. Generally, shell programs can be found in the **/usr/bin** directory, and their filenames end with *sh*.

Some UNIX vendors don't ship the Bourne shell as such; instead, they ship the Korn shell under the filename **sh**.

To see what shells are available on your system, you can try the following command:

```
$ ls /usr/bin/*sh
/usr/bin/csh /usr/bin/ksh /usr/bin/sh
```

The response to the above command line indicates that there are three shells (**csh**, **ksh**, and **sh**) installed on the system. However, you may receive a different response, more like the following:

```
$ ls /usr/bin/*sh
UX: *sh: No such file or directory exists
```

In this instance, the actual shell files may be stored elsewhere on the UNIX filesystem. Check with your system administrator to see where shell files are stored and if you can have access to them.

For the moment, you don't need to know how this command works. Later in this chapter, you'll learn when asterisks (*) can be used on the command line.

At any point in your UNIX usage you can start a new shell. For instance, if you're currently using the C shell and want to switch to the Korn shell, you can enter the following command line:

```
% ksh
$
```

As noted in Chapter 1, the system uses a special character—a *prompt*—to indicate that the system is ready for your input. If you're using the Korn or Bourne shells, your prompt looks like this:

```
$
```

If you're using the C shell, your prompt looks like this:

```
%
```

or

```
spike%
```

where *spike* is the name of the computer. If you're using the Windowing Korn shell, your prompt will look like this:

```
[WKSH]
```

▼

The shell allows you to change your prompt, as the shell controls the character used to designate the prompt. If you're a reformed DOS user, you may want to change the prompt to look more like the DOS prompt (>). In this case (assuming you're a Korn or Bourne shell user), you'd enter the following command in your system:

```
$ PS1="> "
```

This command changes the string $ to the string >, with a space after the > sign. (The space ensures that your commands don't abut the prompt—a move to cut down on potential confusion than anything else.) The quotation marks are used by the system to frame characters to be printed, making sure that the shell knows that the characters within the quotation marks aren't part of the actual command.

In UNIX command lines, characters to be displayed on the screen are bracketed by quotation marks.

The resulting prompt would look like this:

```
>
```

The change to the prompt applies only to your account and won't affect other users. You can use this command line at any point in your daily UNIX usage. However, it applies only to your current computing session; after you log off the system, the prompt will revert to the default.

If you're using the C shell, the following command changes a prompt:

```
% set prompt = "> "
```

▼

In short, the shell controls all interaction between you and the system, but it also allows you to make a lot of changes in the exact interaction. A good example is changing the **Delete** key.

Changing the Delete Key

One of the more useful changes you can make via the shell makes sure that the **Delete** key actually deletes text. Older UNIX systems were rather cavalier regarding the needs of users. Instead of having a designated **Delete** key—no matter what the labels on the keyboard said— these systems would feature awkward key combinations like **Ctrl-H** or **# (Shift-3)**. Using the # character to erase a character gets old quickly; the character is still displayed on your terminal, and if you make numerous typos, you'll have to wade through a lot of # characters to figure out exactly what you typed.

If you can't figure out which key is used to delete a character, or if you just want to make sure that the **Delete** key actually deletes characters, you can actually change the key used to delete characters. This is an old tradition within the UNIX world and is still common today.

To change the delete-character key, use the **stty erase** command line. The usage is simple: Type stty, then a space, then erase, then a space, and then you press the key that you want to delete characters (for our purposes, we'll use the obvious choice of the Del key, although you could use any key on your keyboard if you want). The resulting command line would look like this:

```
$ stty erase [Del]
```

where [*Del*] is the key assigned to the task of deleting characters.

▼

Wildcards

All shells will offer you a lot of flexibility. For instance, the shell allows you to use *wildcards* within a command line. Wildcards are a kind of shorthand that allow you to manipulate multiple commands with a single command. They also allow you to search for files even if you're not quite sure of the specific filename.

There are three UNIX wildcards: *, ?, and [...], as listed in Table 4.1. Each type will be covered in this section.

TABLE 4.1 UNIX WILDCARDS

WILDCARD	MEANING
*	A string of characters.
?	A single character.
[set]	Any character in a series of characters.
[!set]	Any character not in a series of characters.

Though wildcards can be used with any command introduced in Chapters 1–3, you'll find that wildcards are most useful when used with files and directories. You've already seen the * wildcard in action when you looked for the shells located in the **/usr/bin** directory:

```
$ ls /usr/bin/*sh
```

In this instance, you told the shell to list the files in **/usr/bin** that ends in *sh*; the * wildcard specified that any character or characters could precede *sh*.

A more thorough explanation of wildcards is definitely in order. For starters, assume that you're working with the same directory you worked with in Chapter 2:

```
$ ls -a
.              .login        .wastebasket   Preferences    himem.sys
..             .oliniterr    Accessories    Shutdown       mailbox
Xdefaults      .olinitout    Applications   System_Setup   netware
```

132

▼

```
dtfclass       .olinitrc     Disks-etc     Utilities     ramdrive.sys
dtinfo         .olsetup      Folder_Map    Wastebasket   smartdrv.exe
dtprops        .profile      Games         core          windows
lastsession    .sh_history   Help_Desk     data
```

As you'll recall, the **ls -a** command lists all the files in the current directory, including hidden files. There are times when you'll want to list only a portion of the files in the directory. Or you may want to look for a specific file, but you can't remember the name of the file—just that it begins with a specific letter, such as the letter *a*. In this instance, you can use wildcards to hone your searching abilities.

A wildcard character is a substitution for another letter or a series of letters. The asterisk (*), for instance, is a substitute for any other character—no matter how many characters are in the remainder of the filename.

For example, you know that the file you want begins with the letter *a*, but you don't know the rest of the filename. You can combine the asterisk (*) wildcard with the **ls** command to list all files beginning with *a*:

```
$ ls a*
UX:ls: ERROR: Cannot access a*: No such file or directory
```

Gotcha! As you'll recall, case matters in UNIX. As you can see from the earlier listing of the current directory, there are no files or directories that begin with a lowercase *a*. Let's try the command with an uppercase *A*:

```
$ ls A*
Accessories:
Calculator  Clock  Mail  Terminal  Text_Editor
Applications:
DOS  Fingertip_Lib  Win  Win_Setup
```

This tells us that there are two directories beginning with *A* (**Accessories** and **Applications**). How do we know that they are directories? Because the **ls** command listed the subdirectories contained within the directories. However, there are no files in the current directory that begin with an *a*—uppercase or lowercase.

It's clear, then, that your recollection is faulty regarding the filename. You think that the filename may begin with a *d*, and so you use the **ls** command in conjunction with the wildcard *:

```
$ ls d*
data
```

This command shows that there is indeed a file beginning with the letter *d*: **data**.

One important thing to remember when working with the asterisk (*) wildcard: It can also stand for nothing. The following command line and answer is perfectly valid within UNIX:

```
$ ls data*
data
```

Wildcards also work on hidden files if you're using the **ls** command. To generate a listing of hidden files (remember, hidden files begin with a period), use the following command line:

```
$ ls .*
Xdefaults      .dtprops      .oliniterr    .olsetup
dtfclass       .lastsession  .olinitout    .profile
dtinfo         .login        .olinitrc     .sh_history

.:
Accessories   Games        System_Setup   data        ramdrive.sys
Applications  Help_Desk    Utilities      himem.sys   smartdrv.exe
Disks-etc     Preferences  Wastebasket    mailbox     windows
Folder_Map    Shutdown     core           netware

..:
kevin
```

Why all the additional information? Remember: The current directory and the parent directory also begin with periods (. and ..). The contents of the current directory (.) are also listed, as well as the parent directory (..). When there's more than one file or directory that meets the criteria established by the command and the wildcard, the shell will return all such instances, as shown in the following command line:

```
$ ls .ol*
oliniterr .olinitout .olinitrc   .olsetup
```

Because it's so flexible, the asterisk (*) wildcard will probably dominate your wildcard usage. However, there are other types of wildcards that are occasionally useful.

The ? wildcard works similarly to the asterisk (*) wildcard, except for one crucial difference: It matches *only* one character, instead of an unspecified number of characters. Here's an example of the ? wildcard:

```
$ ls file.?
file.1 file.3 file.5 file.8
file.2 file.4 file.7 file.9
```

In this instance, the **ls** command would fail to return filenames with more than one character, such as **file.10** or **file.11**.

Finally, there's the set wildcard. This wildcard allows you to name one or more specific characters to match (such as *a*, *b*, and so on) as well as a range of possible characters (*a–z*, *1–10*). This gives you the greatest control over the characters you want to match with the wildcard, as it allows to you be the most specific.

A few examples should illustrate the set wildcard. To find files in the current directory that end in the letters *c* and *o* (common file suffixes used by programmers), you could use the following command line:

```
$ ls *.[co]
code.c program.c program.o
```

In this case, you asked for filenames where the beginning of the filename could be anything, as long as there was a period in the filename, followed by either a c or an o. To search for filenames that begin with *program* and end with either *c* or *o*, you'd use the following filename:

```
$ ls program.[co]
program.c program.o
```

You can also use the set wildcard to specify a range of characters. For instance, the following command line lists the filenames beginning with *program* and end with any letter between *a* and *f*:

```
$ ls program.[a-f]
```

▼

As always, case counts in UNIX. The previous example would return **program.a**, **program.b**, and so on through **program.f**, but would not return **program.A**, **Program.a**, **PROGRAM.A**, or any variation where all the characters in the filename were not lowercase.

You can also specify characters *not* to be returned by the set wildcard, using an exclamation point (!). For instance, to specify all characters *except* for the letter *a*, you'd use the following command line:

```
$ ls program.[!a]
```

A fuller set of examples using the set wildcard is listed in Table 4.2.

TABLE 4.2 THE SET WILDCARDS IN ACTION

WILDCARD	MEANING
[xyz]	Matches x, y, or z.
[.-_]	Matches ., -, and _.
[a-f]	Matches a, b, and so on through f.
[a-z]	Matches any lowercase letter.
[A-D]	Matches *A*, *B*, *C*, and *D*.
[A-Z]	Matches any uppercase letter.
[a-zA-Z]	Matches any letter.
[!a-z]	Matches any character except lowercase letters.

This is technical

There are some serious drawbacks to the set wildcards. For starters, don't assume that the use of ranges is necessarily accurate on your computer system. The computer *really* doesn't keep track of specific letters and numerals, but rather numerical representations of letters. Because of the different ways different computers keep track of these letters and numerals, the use of sets shouldn't assumed to be totally reliable. You don't need to know why this occurs—unless discussions of ASCII and EBCDIC really excite you—but you should be aware of this fact.

▼

Using Shells

When you login a UNIX system, a file called the *login shell* is immediately run. This file, usually named **.login**, contains some basic information about the specifics regarding your UNIX session. Unless you have a reason to do so, you'll want to leave this file unchanged.

After that (as you'll recall from Chapter 2), the UNIX system places you in your home directory and runs a file called the **.profile** file. This file contains further information about your UNIX usage. A sample **.profile** file—the default **.profile** file from UnixWare, by the way—is as follows.

```
MAIL=/var/mail/${LOGNAME:?}
$HOME/.olsetup   #!@ Do not edit this line !@
```

This **.profile** file doesn't do much. (This has to do with the structures used by UnixWare—a version of UNIX designed for personal computers—and little to do with the actual role of the **.profile** file. Your **.profile** files will probably be longer and more involved.) From it, however, we can see one important aspect to a **.profile** file: How the shell uses variables to customize environments.

Take your time

You have the ability to edit these **.login** and **.profile** files to customize your environment. However, you don't want to be messing with these files at the beginning of your great UNIX journey. Editing these files is for a more experienced view of the UNIX word.

Variables

Those with more than a hazy recollection of their high-school days should recognize a reference to *variables*. In the following line:

```
z=x+y
```

▼

z, *x*, and *y* are all variables. The value of all three can change, depending on input from within the equation or from the reader.

UNIX uses variables the same way: Users can define information with both a name and a value that may change under various circumstances. The shell, in particular, uses variables often. For instance, in the previous section, the example **.profile** file contains the following line:

```
MAIL=/var/mail/${LOGNAME:?}
```

This line sets up the MAIL variable. When the shell or another UNIX application looks for the location to store MAIL, it knows through this variable where to send the information. Variables control the type of terminal you're using, what your system prompt is (as you'll recall, you changed the system prompt earlier in this chapter), and applications that will run right after you login the system.

All of your current variables are set by the system and your system administrator. There may be times when you'll want to change a variable. To do so, you'd use the following command-line syntax:

```
$ VARIABLENAME=VARIABLEVALUE
```

where *VARIABLENAME* is the name of the variable you want to change, and *VARIABLEVALUE* is the new value.

This is technical

One of the most common changes a new user will make involves the *terminal* type. This situation occurs when you're using a terminal different than what the system thinks you're using, resulting in bad communications and errors between your terminal and the system. (You'll see the errors on the screen—it will look like gibberish—and sometimes what you type in the keyboard won't appear accurately on the screen.) While you don't need to know exactly why this variable needs resetting, you should know that you have the power to set it.

To change the terminal variable to the nearly universal VT100 terminal type, using the following command line:

```
$ TERM=vt100
```

▼

The **set** command shows you a listing of your current variables:

```
$ set
CODEPAGE=pc437
CONSEM=no
COUNTRY=1
DESKTOPDIR=/home/kevin
DISPLAY=spike:0.0
DT=yes
HOME=/home/kevin
HZ=100
KEYB=us
LANG=C
LC_CTYPE=C
LC_MESSAGES=C
LC_NUMERIC=C
LC_TIME=C
LD_LIBRARY_PATH=:/usr/X/lib
LOGNAME=kevin
MAIL=/var/mail/kevin
MAILCHECK=600
OPTIND=1
PATH=/usr/bin:/usr/dbin:/usr/ldbin:/usr/X/bin
PS1=$
PS2=>
SHELL=/usr/bin/sh
TERM=xterm
TERMCAP=/etc/termcap
TFADMIN=
TIMEOUT=0
TZ=:US/Central
WINDOWID=29360164
XDM_LOGIN=yes
XGUI=MOTIF
XWINHOME=/usr/X
```

The **set** command is explained in Table 4.3.

▼

TABLE 4.3 COMMAND REFERENCE FOR THE SET COMMAND

> **set** *options*
>
> **PURPOSE**
> The **set** command lists the current variables when it is used with no options. While there are several options available, most are of use to shell programmers or advanced users.
>
> **OPTIONS**
> **-a**   Exports changes to variables.

Some C shell users can use the same command. However, the output will look different:

```
spike% set
argv    ()
cwd     /home/kevin
path    (/usr/bin /usr/dbin /usr/ldbin /usr/X/bin)
prompt spike%
shell   /bin/csh
status 0
term    xterm
```

If the **set** command doesn't work on your system, try using **setenv** or **env**.

```
% env
CODEPAGE=pc437
CONSEM=no
COUNTRY=1
DESKTOPDIR=/home/kevin
DISPLAY=spike:0.0
DT=yes
HOME=/home/kevin
```

```
HZ=100
KEYB=us
LANG=C
LC_CTYPE=C
LC_MESSAGES=C
LC_NUMERIC=C
LC_TIME=C
LD_LIBRARY_PATH=:/usr/X/lib
LOGNAME=kevin
MAIL=/var/mail/kevin
PATH=/usr/bin:/usr/dbin:/usr/ldbin:/usr/X/bin
SHELL=/usr/bin/sh
TERM=xterm
TERMCAP=/etc/termcap
TFADMIN=
TIMEOUT=0
TZ=:US/Central
WINDOWID=29360164
XDM_LOGIN=yes
XGUI=MOTIF
XWINHOME=/usr/X
PWD=/home/kevin
```

There are a few lines in the previous examples that at first glance seem to be in error, such as:

PATH=/usr/bin:/usr/dbin:/usr/ldbin:/usr/X/bin

This is not an error. Rather, the variable encompasses more than one item. In this case, the PATH variable tells the shell where to look for filenames. Since there is more than one directory containing commands, the system is set up to look in more than one directory. In this example, colons (:) are used to distinguish between multiple options.

The **env** command is explained in Table 4.4.

TABLE 4.4 COMMAND REFERENCE FOR THE ENV COMMAND

env *option [variable=value] command*

PURPOSE

The **env** command displays the current user environment variables with their values, or make changes to environment variables for users of the C shell.

OPTION

-          Ignores the current environment variable.

All in all, there's a lot of information you'll need to wade through when using the **set/setenv/env** commands. Most of it will be utterly meaningless to you. (In the previous examples, most of the information involved the specific needs of UnixWare.) However, there are a few shell variables that you should know about, and they are listed in Tables 4.5 and 4.6.

TABLE 4.5 SHELL VARIABLES FOR THE BOURNE AND KORN SHELLS

VARIABLE	MEANING
CDPATH	Directories that are automatically searched when you use the **cd** command.
HOME	The full name of your home directory.
LOGNAME	Your login name.
MAIL	The directory where your electronic-mail messages are stored.
PATH	Directories that are automatically searched by the shell when you issue a command to the system.
SHELL	The full filename of your current shell.
TERM	Your terminal type.
TZ	Your current time zone.
USER	Your login name (used instead of LOGNAME on some systems).

TABLE 4.6 SHELL VARIABLES FOR THE C SHELL

cdpath	Directories that are automatically searched when you use the **cd** command.
HOME	The full name of your home directory.
mail	The directory where your electronic-mail messages are stored.
PATH	Directories that are automatically searched by the shell when you issue a command to the system.
prompt	Sets the characters used in the prompt.
TERM	Your terminal type.
USER	Your login name (used instead of LOGNAME on some systems).

When working with variables, there are a few things to remember:

▲ Remember at all times: *case counts*. TERM, Term, and term would be three different variables. All the system's reserved variables all are in uppercase letters.

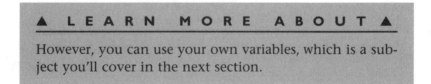

▲ **L E A R N   M O R E   A B O U T** ▲

However, you can use your own variables, which is a subject you'll cover in the next section.

▲ When using a variable on the command line, you must preface it with a dollar sign ($), as you did earlier in this chapter while checking for the shell currently in use:

```
$ echo $SHELL
/usr/bin/ksh
```

The dollar sign ($) tells the shell that you're specifying a variable on the command line, rather than a command or an option to a command.

▼

The above use of the **echo** command can be used to check for the value of any variable. Instead of wading through the information returned by the **set** command when looking for a specific variable, you can simply use **echo**, as in the following:

```
$ echo $TERM
xterm
```

Setting Your Own Variables

You aren't limited to the variables initially supported by the system. While the notion of setting up your own variables seems too complicated, there are several situations where you will find that your own variables are very convenient.

For instance: You're working on an involved project and want to store all of the files in the same directory, buried deep within the directory tree:

/users/kevin/data/reports/research/1994.

This is a mighty long directory name to type every time you want to store or call a file. In this case, you can assign a variable to this long directory name. To do so, you'd use the following command line:

```
$ DATA="/users/kevin/data/reports/research/1994"
```

Here, the use of the DATA variable is totally arbitrary: You could use variable names of REPORTS or FILES, as long as the name you choose isn't already being used by the system.

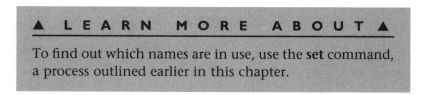

▲ **L E A R N   M O R E   A B O U T** ▲

To find out which names are in use, use the **set** command, a process outlined earlier in this chapter.

▼

In the previous command line, you'll notice that the name of the directory was in quotation marks. Any string you save as a variable must be placed in quotation marks.

Exporting Variables

When you create a variable, you're making sure it can be used by the shell. Similarly, when you change a system variable, you're making the change to the shell. In both cases, you're not necessarily applying the change to any applications you're using.

To make sure that your changes can be used throughout your UNIX computing experience, use the **export** command:

```
$ export DATA
```

You can export multiple variables on the same command line:

```
$ export DATA TERM PATH
```

When you assign your own variable, you can also export it on the same command line:

```
$ DATA="/users/kevin/reports/research/1994"; export data
```

If you're exporting every variable you assign or change, you can use an option to the **set** command to make these assignments automatic:

```
$ set -a
```

▼

Removing Your Variables

If you are finished with variables, you can remove them from the system with the **unset** command:

```
$ unset DATA
```

This removes variables defined by DATA.

TABLE 4.7 COMMAND REFERENCE FOR THE UNSET COMMAND

unset *variable*

PURPOSE

The **unset** command literally unsets variables set by the user or the system.

OPTIONS

None.

Standard Input/Output

When you use commands like **set** and **unset**, the results of the command are automatically displayed to your monitor. Generally speaking, UNIX assumes that commands are entered from the keyboard (known as *standard input*), with the results displayed to the monitor (known as *standard output*). Together, standard input and standard output is commonly referred to as *I/O*. This reliance on jargon is a typically obtuse—typical for UNIX, at least—way of saying

▼

that things you type with the keyboard will appear on-screen. (Doesn't jargon suck?)

So put the jargon behind you and focus on the relatively simple concepts underlying standard input/output. There are times when you'll want a command to receive input from another source (such as a file), and there are times when you'll want a command to send output to a place other than the monitor, such as a printer or a file. In these cases, you'll want to *redirect* the input or output. This redirection is performed as part of the command line and is quite simple to accomplish.

In fact, you'll find the ability to redirect input and output to be one of the handiest functions of the UNIX operating system. Unfortunately, this ability is generally ignored by beginning users, who tend to be put off by all of the jargon associated with a very basic functionality—who would think that something appearing in the documentation as standard *input/output redirection* or *redirection I/O* could be so simple?

UNIX uses the > and < characters to accomplish this simple redirection. For instance, you may want to save the results of the **ls** command to a file instead of the screen. This is probably the most common usage of redirection, since the information generated by many UNIX commands tends to run on the largish side, to say the least. Trying to pick a piece of information from rapidly scrolling text can be difficult, and it's much easier to save the information to a file and search through it with a text editor.

To send the results of the **ls** command to a file named *myfile* instead of the screen, you'd use the following command line:

```
$ ls > myfile
```

That's all there is to it. This will work with any command that sends its output to the screen. Once you have the results in a file, you can use any number of UNIX tools to view that information at a more leisurely pace—Chapter 3 covers many such tools.

There are other redirection tools, as explained in Table 4.8.

▼

TABLE 4.8 SHELL REDIRECTION COMMANDS

Symbol	Usage	Result
>	*command>filename*	The output of the command *command* is sent to *filename*.
<	*command<filename*	The input from *filename* is used by *command*.
>>	*command>>filename*	The output from *command* is appended to *filename*.
|	*command1|command2*	First *command1* is run, and then the output is sent to *command2*.

Using some of the commands you used in Chapter 3, you'll see more clearly the redirection in action in Table 4.9.

TABLE 4.9 REDIRECTION IN ACTION

Command	Result
ls > *filename*	The contents of the current directory, as listed with the ls command, are sent to *filename* rather than displayed on the screen.
	If *filename* doesn't exist, the shell will create it. If *filename* does exist, the results of the **ls** command will overwrite the existing data.
	In this instance, information from the **ls** command is used as input for the file *filename*.
cat <*filename*	The **cat** command displays the contents of the file *filename* on the screen. In this instance, *filename* is used as input for the **cat** command.

▼

ls >>*filename*	The contents of the current directory, as listed with the **ls** command, are appended to the end of the file *filename*. In this instance, information from the **ls** command is used as input for the file *filename*.
ls | lp	The contents of the current directory, as listed with the **ls** command, are sent to the UNIX command **lp**, which prints the information.

▲ **L E A R N   M O R E   A B O U T** ▲

You will learn more about the **lp** command later in this chapter.

Reality Check: Redirection

UNIX does not like beginning or casual users. This is evident by the harm that can be caused by the seemingly innocent act of redirection.

What makes UNIX so unfeeling? Because it will wipe out files at the drop of a hat. For instance, if you use the following command:

```
$ ls > myfile
```

and there already existed a file named *myfile* in the directory, UNIX would have no qualms about wiping out the old *myfile* and replacing it with the new *myfile*. In UNIX jargon, the old file was clobbered (for once, the jargon is illuminating).

Pipes

The idea of *pipes* takes redirection to a new level of functionality, but also to a new level of complexity. While there are certainly times when pipes are convenient, don't worry if you're so intimidated by them that you never use them.

▼

A pipe acts as a conduit between two commands. With a pipe, you specify that the results of one command should be used as the input of a second command. In a sense, the pipe is a temporary file that holds data after it's been acted upon by one command and before it is used by a second command.

Setting up a *pipeline* is a simple matter:

```
$ command1 | command2
```

In this example, the output from *command1* is used as input for *command2*. The character in the middle is a vertical bar. (Aha! *This* is why that funny-looking character exists on keyboards!) While this example is limited to only two commands, there's no limit as to how many commands you can set up in a pipeline.

Most often, pipes—as well as redirection—are used when printing documents with the **lp** command. The **lp** command is the UNIX command for printing.

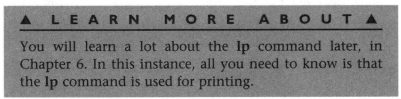

▲ **L E A R N   M O R E   A B O U T** ▲

You will learn a lot about the **lp** command later, in Chapter 6. In this instance, all you need to know is that the **lp** command is used for printing.

Let's say you want to print the contents of a directory after generating them with the **ls** command. There are two ways to do it. You could generate the listing and then redirect the output to a file, and then you can print the file. There's nothing particularly wrong with this method, although it uses two steps to perform what should be a simple task. (It also has you creating a file, which means you must make sure and delete the file at some point.) Or you can directly print the results of the **ls** command using a pipe, as in the following command line:

```
$ ls | lp
```

There's no limit as to how many commands you connect with pipes.

▼

Passwords and Usernames

In Chapter 1, you ran through a typical login session assuming that the system administrator had set up your account and password. There may be times when you choose your own password—as well as situations where you'll want to choose your own password and username.

Indeed, if you have a particularly gracious system administrator, you'll be able to choose your own username before an account is opened for you. There's nothing particularly mystical about usernames, but there are a few things to remember when choosing one. Your username must be more than two characters, and usually not more than eight characters. (You've already seen this restriction blown out of the water with the earlier example of *kreichard* as a username.) It must be based on your real name in some way, however, especially if your system is connected to the Internet: Choosing a username of *lord_galacticon* may be cute, but if you try that crap on the Internet, you'll receive no respect.

However, choosing a password isn't a trifling matter. Indeed, sloppy passwords are one of the prime reasons why security breaches occur in UNIX systems. And you don't want to be responsible for some little hack causing problems to your computer system. Keep that in mind as you choose a password, as well as these factors:

▲ Make sure your password is longer than six characters. Shorter passwords are easier to decipher by either random chance or determined individuals.

▲ Your password must contain two alphabetic characters and one numeral or special character (!, @, #, etc.), generally speaking. Some older UNIX systems, however, don't allow the use of nonalphabetic characters, and some PC-based UNIX systems, such as UnixWare, don't require a numeral. If you're trying to enter a new password and the system won't accept it, check with your system administrator.

▲ *Never* use a password based solely on personal information. A popular tool for system hackers is to try personal names as passwords, on the theory that someone would have entered their lover's name as a password. In addition,

▼

don't use your middle name, your spouse's name, or your job title as a password.

▲ Don't use words that are easily guessed, such as **sun**, **boss**, **password**, or anything else obvious.

▲ On the other hand, don't make your password too complicated. This is a string that you'll need to remember, after all—if you make it too complex, you'll probably just write it on a sheet of paper and leaving it next to your terminal, which means that anyone walking by your terminal can probably see your password. (Indeed, this author has seen instances where users wrote their passwords on Post-It notes and then attached the Post-It note to the terminal screen.) The best advice is to use two easily remembered words in combination, making sure that the two portions of the password aren't related. For instance, you may think Rush Limbaugh is full of hot air, you choose *rush* and *hot* as elements for your password. This isn't a valid password—remember, you need at least one numeral—but a password of *rushhot1* certainly would be. (*Rushhotair1* would be an even better password.)

There's a neat trick used by many UNIX users over the years that turns passwords into gibberish, but still keeps them easy to remember. Choose a word or phrase that means something to you, like **passion**. Now look at your keyboard. For your real password, use the keys to the upper-left of the keys spelling out **passion**. In this case, the first letter of *passion*, *p*, becomes *0*, and *passion* becomes *0qww89h*, your real password. No one is going to ever hack *0qww89h* as a password.

Changing Your Password

It's not unusual to have to change your password. In fact, some system administrators force their users to change their passwords regularly in order to increase security.

▼

This capability is actually built into the UNIX operating system; the system administrator can tell the system to force users to change passwords every so often.

In this instance, passwords are said to *age* and must be replaced every so often. In addition, you may want to change your password from the password originally assigned by the system administrator when your account was installed.

There's no such thing as total privacy on a UNIX system. Passwords are stored in a central location and in such a manner that the system administrator has the power to see a list of these passwords.

To change your password, use the **passwd** command. This command is rather simple: After you login the system, you run the command and enter the new information when requested:

```
$ passwd
UX: passwd: changing password for kevin
Old password:
New password:
Re-enter new password:
$
```

As when entering your password, when logging in the system, the **passwd** doesn't display your password as you enter it.

Table 4.10 summarizes the **passwd** command.

TABLE 4.10 COMMAND REFERENCE FOR THE PASSWD COMMAND

passwd *options*

passwd *options user* (privileged users)

PURPOSE

The **passwd** command sets or changes your password.

OPTIONS

-s   Displays current password information:

user	User name.
status	Password status: **NP** (no password), **PS** (password), or **LK** (locked).
mm/dd/yy	Date when last changed.
min	Minimum number of days before password must be changed.
max	Maximum number of days before password must be changed.
notice	Number of days before you are given notice that your password must be changed.

The -s option is available only in the newest versions of UNIX.

SCO UNIX users have one additional option to the **passwd** command: You can have the system randomly generate a password for you if you prefer. In addition, the system will also ask you if you want a pronounceable password.

Many users confuse the **pwd** command with the **passwd** command. As you'll recall, the **pwd** command returns the name of the current working directory.

This Chapter in Review

▲ The shell is an intermediary between you and the UNIX operating system. As such, it has a lot of power in your daily computing chores.

▲ There are many different shells available. The three most popular shells are the C shell, the Bourne shell, and the Korn shell.

▲ To let you know that it is ready for input, the shell displays a prompt on the screen. The characters used for the prompt are specific to the shell. You also have ability to create a new prompt at any time.

▲ Wildcards allows you to shorten command lines by substituting a single character for a wide range of characters. In addition, other wildcards can be used to represent a specified range of characters.

▲ Standard input/output and redirection allow you to change where the input and output of commands are sent. For instance, redirection allows you to send the results of the **ls** command to a file instead of the screen.

▲ A pipe allows you to specify that the output from one command be the input for another command. While this isn't a feature you'll use often, it is quite convenient—especially when you're printing files.

▲ Though a system administrator probably set up your password before you ever logged on your UNIX system, you still have the ability to change your password at all times with the **passwd** command.

▪ CHAPTER FIVE ▪
Communications, Networking, and Electronic Mail

One of the biggest benefits to using the UNIX operating system is its ability to communicate with other computer systems, which may or may not be running UNIX. In this chapter, you'll learn about networking and communicating with other users and other computer systems with the following methods:

- ▲ Learning who else is logged on your system with the **who** command.
- ▲ Chatting directly with other users with the **write** and **talk** commands.
- ▲ Extending your network with electronic mail.
- ▲ Using the **mail** command to send and read mail.
- ▲ Using the Internet.
- ▲ Managing your incoming electronic mail.
- ▲ Figuring out how Internet addresses work.
- ▲ Reading through Usenet newsgroup.
- ▲ Learning how to use a text editor with the **mail** command.
- ▲ Grabbing files from remote systems with the **ftp** command.
- ▲ Using anonymous ftp to login remote systems.
- ▲ Uncompressing files with the **uncompress** and **unpack** commands.

You'll Never Walk Alone

When companies decide to go with the UNIX operating system, a prime consideration in the decision-making process was probably UNIX's ability to easily interconnect computers throughout a company or even in more than one location. You were exposed to this feature in Chapter 1, when you learned about a UNIX network.

As a user, you'll benefit from UNIX connectivity (to use the fancy term the computer professionals use). Depending on your system, you can use UNIX's networking capabilities to communicate with other users within your company, as well as computer users across the world.

This is technical

Networking is simultaneously one of the simplest and most complex concepts associated with the UNIX operating system. Networking is complex in that the actual mechanisms for setting up networking tend to be obscure and arcane. But networking is also simple for the end user, who shouldn't worry about why things work, but rather how to do them. To send electronic mail, you shouldn't need to worry about leased-line access to the Internet, TCP/IP, and the **sendmail** program; you only need to know what program allows you to send electronic mail and how to use it. Don't be awed by the amount of technical jargon that occurs in discussions of UNIX communications; just plow through and use the tools. When in doubt, let your system administrator deal with the technical aspects of networking.

Communicating With Other Local Users

There's no law that says a UNIX network must be connected to the rest of the world through the Internet. Indeed, many companies choose not to connect their UNIX networks to the Internet, or do so in a limited fashion. This limitation doesn't affect your ability to send and receive electronic messages from other users on your own company network, however. You'll see this through a few UNIX commands devoted to communications within the network.

First, you'll need to know exactly what users are currently logged on the UNIX system. You can do this with the **who** command.

```
$ who
kevin    term/10   May 1 10:11
geisha   term/07   May 1 07:32
```

As you can see, there's a lot of information returned by this command—the users on the system, the terminals they are using, and when they logged in—but most of it is relatively worthless to you. The only thing you need to know from this listing is the usernames of the people logged on the system.

The **who** comand is explained more fully in Table 5.1.

TABLE 5.1 COMMAND REFERENCE FOR THE WHO COMMAND

who *options file*

PURPOSE
The **who** command displays the names and other information about users logged on the system.

OPTIONS

am I	Displays who you are (your system name).
-a	Uses all available options.
-b	Returns the last time and date the system was booted.
-H	Inserts column headings.
-q	Quick who, which displays only usernames.
-s	Returns name, line, and time fields (default).

▼

On larger systems, you'll find that the information returned by the **who** command is quite voluminous. If you're not sure of your login information, use the **whoamI** command, which is actually a variation on the **who** command:

```
$ who am I
Kevin
```

The **who am I** command is not available on all UNIX systems.

With this information, you can send an instant message to anyone on the system with the **write** command. You see by the **who** command that *geisha* is logged on the system. UNIX allows you to send instant messages on the network to anyone else logged on the system. These messages will be seen only by the message recipient. To alert *geisha* that you want to electronically communicate, you'd use the following command line:

```
$ write geisha
```

This command causes a message to pop up on geisha's terminal and rings the terminal's bell. If *geisha* wanted to converse, she types the following command line on her terminal:

```
$ write yourname
```

where *yourname* is your username. You can send messages back and forth over the network from that point on. If you're using a character-based terminal, sending messages is about the only thing you'll be able to do. If you're using a graphical interface and sending messages with an *xterm* inside its own window, you can also do other work while you're sending messages back and forth.

When you are done with your message, type **o-o** (short for *over-and-out*), and then press **Ctrl-D** or the **Delete** key to stop the interaction.

Table 5.2 summarizes the **write** command.

TABLE 5.2 COMMAND REFERENCE FOR THE WRITE COMMAND

write *username*

PURPOSE
The **write** command sends a text message to another user. Use **Ctrl-D** or the **Delete** key to exit.

OPTIONS
None.

If you are using a newer version of UNIX, you may have available a new and improved version of **write**, called **talk**.

The **talk** command refines the **write** command and makes it easier to use. Essentially, the **talk** command divides the screen into two parts. The top half of the screen displays your messages sent over the network, while the bottom half of the screen displays the responses.

The following command line starts a chat session with *geisha*:

```
$ talk geisha
```

Geisha will see a similar message on her screen:

```
Message from Talk_Daemon@spike at 4:30
talk: connection requested by kevin@spike
talk: respond with: talk kevin@spike
```

where *kevin* is your logname and *spike* is your machine name. If *geisha* were in a chatty mood, she could respond and start a chat session with the following:

```
$ talk kevin@spike
```

At this point, the **talk** command divides your screen into two halves.

When you're done chatting, press the **Delete** key.

Table 5.3 summarizes the **talk** command.

▼

TABLE 5.3 COMMAND REFERENCE FOR THE TALK COMMAND

talk *username[@hostname]*

PURPOSE

The **talk** command allows you to converse with another user on the network. The command splits your screen into two areas: The top half contains your typing, while the bottom contains messages from the other user. Use **Ctrl-D** or the **Delete** key to exit.

OPTIONS

username   The other user.

There may be times when you don't want to chat with another user—your boss is in the office or you're on the phone with an important client.

In these cases, you'll want to turn away the request to chat with the **mesg** command:

```
$ mesg n
```

This command line turns away all requests generated by the **write** or **talk** commands. The user initiating the chat would see the following on the screen:

```
Permission denied
```

When your boss leaves and you want to waste the rest of your day chatting with other users, you can use the following command line:

```
$ mesg y
```

The **mesg** command is summarized in Table 5.4.

TABLE 5.4 COMMAND REFERENCE FOR THE MESG COMMAND

mesg *options*

PURPOSE
The **mesg** command allows or denies permission to other users
to send you messages via the **write** or **talk** commands.

OPTIONS
-n   Forbids messages.
-y   Allows messages.

Electronic Mail: Extending Your Network

Sending electronic mail to individuals, groups of people, or everyone
in your company surely isn't the flashiest feature found in the UNIX
operating system, but it's surely one of the most-used features. Other
networking systems—such as the popular DOS network software,
NetWare—lack the basic ability to manage electronic mail and do so
only after the addition of more expensive third-party packages, like
cc:Mail or Microsoft *Mail*.

Indeed, electronic-mail capabilities have been an important part of
UNIX since its humble beginnings. As UNIX has evolved, so has electronic mail—especially popular electronic-mail UNIX programs like
mail, **mailx**, **mush**, **Mail**, and **elm**. While the exact procedures differ
from program to program, the concepts underlying UNIX electronic
mail remain the same. In this chapter, the **mail** and **mailx** programs
will be used to illustrate electronic mail. While your electronic-mail
package may differ on some of the details, broadly speaking, it should
work similarly to the steps outlined in this chapter.

▼

You won't need to set up or configure your **mail** program, no matter what it may be. Check with your system administrator about the specific steps you'll use to send and receive mail on your system.

This is technical

Receiving Your Mail

When you login your system, you are told whether or not you have electronic mail waiting for you. If there is mail waiting, you'll see a line like the following:

```
You have mail.
```

This message will appear every time you login and there is mail waiting for you, as the shell is normally set up to remind you that there's electronic mail waiting.

Command

To view this mail, you'll use the **mail** command:

```
$ mailx
mail version 4.2  Type ? for help
"/var/mail/kevin": 1 message 1 new
>N 1 kevin Wed May 18 15:18  12/227 stuff
?
```

As you can see, the system lists your electronic-mail messages in the order they were received by the system, newest mail first. The listings include the sender of the mail (in this case, *kevin*), the time and date the message was received (*Wed May 19 15:18*), the number of lines in

▼

the message and the size of the message in bytes (*12/227*), and the subject of the message (*stuff*).

If you want to read the first message listed, you'd press the **Enter** key. The entire text of the message will scroll by—probably too fast for you to read on the fly. To read a portion at a time, type **Ctrl-S**; to start the scrolling again, type **Ctrl-Q**.

In this case, there are two electronic-mail messages waiting for you. The first, from *geisha*, was sent to you from within your own system. The second, from *kreichard@mcimail.com*, was sent from outside your system. How can you tell the difference?

Simple. If your UNIX system is connected to the Internet, you can send and receive electronic-mail messages from around the world. Mail from other systems has its own unique addressing scheme, seen here by the foreign-looking *kreichard@mcimail.com*. Mail from your own system uses the same usernames that have been explained throughout this book. Assuming your username is *geisha* and your UNIX system name is *spike*, a message sent to another user within your own system would be from *geisha*, but a message sent over the Internet would be from *geisha@spike.com*.

The ampersand (**&**) at the end of the mail is the prompt for the **mail** program. Many UNIX commands have their own prompt. This is to make sure that you know that anything you type is meant as input for the command and not for the system as a whole.

After you've read through the messages, there are a number of actions to take by entering a letter at the **mail** command prompt. The important actions are listed in Table 5.5.

▼

TABLE 5.5 MAIL COMMANDS AT THE MAIL PROMPT

COMMAND	ACTION
Return key	Displays the next message.
-	Displays the previous message.
?	Lists available commands.
n	Displays message *n*, where *n* is the number of a message.
d	Deletes current message; if you don't delete the message, it will be stored in the UNIX system and referred to every time you use the **mail** command.
f *file*	Read mail messages in *file*.
h	Displays a list of messages in your mailbox.
m *address*	Creates a mail message and sends it to the electronic-mail *address*.
n	Displays the next message.
p	Redisplays the current message.
q	Quits **mail**.
r	Replies to the sender of the current message.
R	Replies to the sender of the current message, as well as other recipients of the message.
s *file*	Saves the full message to the filename *file*; if no filename is specified, the message is saved to **$HOME/mbox**.
u *n*	Undeletes message number *n*.
w *file*	Saves the message sans header to the filename *file*; if no filename is specified, the message is saved to **$HOME/mbox**.
x	Quits **mail**, but does so without deleting the messages you deleted.

Saving Your Messages

Once you've received a message, you'll probably want to save it for future reference. To do so, you need only type *s* at the **mail** command prompt:

```
? s
```

If you don't specify a filename, the system will automatically append the message to the file **$HOME/mbox**. If you don't receive many messages, it's no big deal to combine your messages into one large file. However, if you receive many mail messages on a variety of topics, then you'll want to put a little more thought into organizing your mail messages. For instance, if you're corresponding with an important client—let's say the giant computer firm HAL—you may want to save all of this correspondence to a single file, say, named **HAL**. To do so, use the following **mail** command line after you read a message from a HAL executive:

```
? s HAL
```

When you do this the first time, the **mail** program creates a file named **HAL**. After that, the **mail** program will append messages to the existing **HAL** file. To read this file, use the *-f* option to the **mail** command:

```
$ mail -f HAL
```

When you save your electronic mail to a file, don't assume that the file is private, either technically or morally. The system administrator has the power to read **$HOME/mbox** and can override any file protections you may set up on the file. In addition, the courts have held that electronic-mail messages are not automatically private correspondence, and as such can be read at any time by company officials. While you shouldn't be using company resources for personal use—and we all know *that* never happens, nudge, nudge, wink, wink— be warned *that* you should remove any incriminating evidence should you do the unspeakable.

The Internet: Mail Around the World

The Internet has been a trendy subject in the media recently, as the world continues its fascination with high technology. While this book would never stoop to the level of trendmongering, it's clear that you can benefit from the various Internet offerings.

The Internet is an amorphous collection of computers around the world, networked to send information instantaneously from one location on the network to another. There's no central location to the Internet, no place for people to call or get more information.

Still, the Internet has managed to become the most extensive computer communications network in the world. Many corporations, universities, and research institutions send and receive mail using the Internet. While not every computer on the Internet uses the UNIX operating system (indeed, every type of computer, from PCs to Cray supercomputers, are represented), UNIX-based computers play an important role on the Internet.

However, the idea of the Internet is *so* amorphous that it's best for you not to try to figure out its structure or how it works. You don't need to know these things to actually use the Internet. As a user, you don't need to know a recipient's electronic-mail address; your system administrator handles the sometimes-messy details of connecting to the Internet. Indeed, you're best off knowing exactly what the Internet can do and how you can achieve these offerings with your own system. Unfortunately, the exact mechanisms you use to connect to the Internet will depend on your system, as there are literally dozens and dozens of UNIX programs used to send and receive electronic mail, as well as browsing through portions of the Internet.

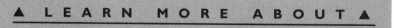

▲ L E A R N   M O R E   A B O U T ▲

In this chapter, you'll be exposed to the basic UNIX tools for sending and receiving electronic mail, as well as to the most popular tools for Internet access.

As you read through this chapter, remember one thing: The exact mechanisms detailed in this chapter aren't as important as the concepts they illustrate.

Internet Offerings

Broadly speaking, there are three major portions to the Internet. Each will be introduced in this section and then explained further.

Electronic Mail

Perhaps the most popular portion of the Internet concerns electronic mail, which you've already learned about earlier in this chapter. Mail messages can be a simple text message, or they can have a file attached. The focus of this chapter is electronic mail, either on the Internet or internally.

Usenet Newsgroups

When people say they were reading through messages on the Internet, they were really reading through messages on the Usenet. These messages are contained in newsgroups, which are electronic discussions organized around a single topic. There are hundreds of newsgroups, but you can choose the newsgroups that best match your interests. How you actually read and access newsgroups will depend on your specific system setup, though you'll probably use one of these popular Usenet browsing tools: **readnews**, **vnews**, **rn**, **xrn**, or **nn**. Again, check with your system administrator as to the exact newsreader your system uses, and what newsgroups are available.

Some popular newsgroups are listed in Table 5.6.

TABLE 5.6 A SAMPLING OF USENET NEWSGROUPS

NEWSGROUP	TOPIC
alt.barney.dinosaur.die.die.die	The name pretty much sums it up.
alt.bizarre.sex	Bizarre sex.
rec.arts.wobegon	A discussion of "A Prairie Home Companion".
rec.food.drink.beer	A discussion of beer.
rec.music.rem	The music of REM.
soc.culture.indian.telugu	A discussion of the Telugu people of India.

Reality Check: The Usenet

There's a lot to be said for the Usenet, particularly in specialized news-groups related to academic and computer-related topics. The more specific the discussion, the more information you can glean from it. As a UNIX beginner, there are quite a few Usenet UNIX-specific newsgroups—even one devoted to UNIX beginners—that you'll find interesting, and they are listed in the appendix.

Most Usenet users, however, don't bother with discussions about the UNIX operating system (their loss). Generally speaking, the more general the discussion, the more crap you'll be forced to wade through. Take this shining—and unedited—example of Usenet knowledge, which was posted to a newsgroup devoted to a discussion of *Wired* magazine:

> *you can multiply your iq (heretofore based upon print literacy) by a factor of ten simply by placing two tv sets side by side, tuned to two different channels, volume up on both, and concentrating on*

following the information flux simultaneously. within ten minutes of moderate concentration you will have eclipsed 500 years of obsolete sequential print patterning. multi-screen image literacy will position your perceptions within a flux of simultaneous info, ie., a more accurate model of the real 3-d world of simultaneous events.

Everyone is welcome to their own opinions, and I wouldn't argue that the poster should not have made this "contribution" to cognitive research. The distressing thing was that several people saw it fit to take it seriously in a rather involved discussion (that is, there were 30 or so messages arguing the merits of the original post). Use this example as a telling detail regarding the high level of discourse on the Usenet.

Remote Access

When you have full access to the Internet, you can upload and download files as if they were stored on your computer system. This ability also allows you to look at a remote computer in the same manner you look at your own: You can generate a listing of directory contents with the **ls** command, for instance.

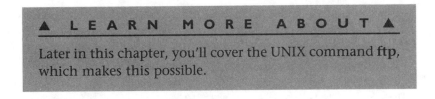

▲ L E A R N   M O R E   A B O U T ▲

Later in this chapter, you'll cover the UNIX command **ftp**, which makes this possible.

Internet Addresses

Throughout this chapter you've seen references to *kreichard@mcimail.com*, which happens to be the electronic-mail address for this book's author. It is typical of an Internet mail address. Essentially, there are three parts to this address, as illustrated in Figure 5.1.

Figure 5.1 An electronic-mail address parsed

In this instance, *kreichard* is the logname or username. If this were your electronic-mail address, your logname or username would appear in its place.

The last part of the address, the *domain name*, is a unique destination within the greater Internet world. This scheme grew out of the need for international standardization of electronic-mail addresses and provides a hierarchical structure to addressing. Essentially, the world is divided into country domains, although our sample address doesn't illustrate this—where there's no country domain listed, the country is assumed to be the United States. (Remember, Americans assume they are the center of the universe.) These country domains are then divided into educational domains (indicated by the suffix *.edu* in the address) and commercial domains (indicated by the suffix *.com* in the address).

In the case of our sample address, we know that it refers to a commercial entity, indicated by the suffix *.com*. *Mcimail* refers to the specific commercial entity; in this case, the reference is to MCI Mail, a popular electronic-mail service. (Yes, the world is indeed getting smaller. Commercial services like MCI Mail and CompuServe can communicate directly with Internet users.) In this context, you could also say that the *machine name* is *mcimail*.

The @ symbol (referred to as *at* when read aloud) separates the two portions of the address.

This electronic-mail addressing method is not the only method. It is, however, the most popular method. If you see an electronic-mail address like this:

```
uunet!concubune!kevin
```

don't be disconcerted. This is an older method of electronic-mail addressing called a *bang path*. Just use it like you'd use other electronic-mail addresses used in this chapter.

If you're not sure of your machine name, you can use the **uname** command with the *-n* option:

```
$ uname -n
spike
```

Chances are pretty good that your machine name is not *spike*; your machine name is guaranteed to be different.

Sending Mail

Armed with the electronic-mail address of a recipient, you're set and ready to send electronic mail using your electronic-mail software. You can send mail at any time; just like regular mail, the recipient doesn't need to be at home (that is, logged on their computer) to receive electronic mail. (As with your UNIX system, mail messages are stored by systems until they can be retrieved by the user.) And, as you'll see, it's very easy to send electronic mail.

The examples with this section will be illustrated by use of the **mail** command. Your specific mail package may differ. Check with your system administrator.

To send electronic mail, you'll use the aforementioned **mail** command. In this example command line, you're sending electronic mail to *kreichard@mcimail.com*:

```
$ mail kreichard@mcimail.com
```

Since there's a domain name listed in the address, you can assume that this particular message is meant for a computer user on the Internet. If the mail is meant for a user on your own system, you can omit the domain name.

The **mail** program will then take over, asking you to supply various bits of information. For starters, you'll be asked to supply the subject of the message.

No, you won't fail any tests if your subject doesn't *exactly* match text of your message.

The request for the subject will look like this:

```
Subject:
```

Type in the subject and then press the **Return** key.

At this point, type your message. Don't worry about pressing **Return** at the end of every line; the system will automatically wrap the text to fit the width of your screen. When you're done with a paragraph, you can press **Return** and continue typing on the following line.

When you're finished with your message, hit the **Return** key and make sure the cursor is on its own line. At this point, type **Ctrl-D**, the UNIX command for end-of-file.

If you've been paying attention, you'll have noticed that almost every command uses **Ctrl-D** to end data entry.

At this point the prompt should return.

By the time you're finished, your message should look like this:

```
$ mail kreichard@mcimail.com
Subject: Great book!
I have learned so much from this book. UNIX is still a mystery,
but I feel empowered by this book.
^D
$
```

This procedure assumes that you want to go ahead and send the electronic mail. If you begin a mail message and decide not to send it, type **~q** (the tilde character followed by the letter q) at the beginning of a line. However, this command is worthless after you type **Ctrl-D**—the message is gone forever at that point.

▼

You can also send messages to multiple users with the **mail** command and the *-t* option:

```
$ mail -t kevin geisha spike
```

Finally, you can use the **mail** command to send files that you've already created. In many ways, this is the most effective way of sending a message, in that you can create a coherent electronic-mail message and take the time to edit it before sending it off. To start with, you must actually create the body of the message using a text editor like **vi** or **emacs**.

After saving the file and quitting the text editor, you'll use the created file as input using redirection, which you learned about in Chapter 4:

```
$ mail kreichard.mcimail.com < file
```

where *file* is the name of the file you created with the text editor.

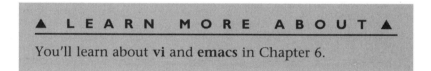

▲ L E A R N   M O R E   A B O U T ▲

You'll learn about **vi** and **emacs** in Chapter 6.

Special Circumstances for Sending Mail

Depending on the version of UNIX you're using, there are two useful options available.

If you are using Berkeley UNIX or a derivative (or a hybrid, like UnixWare), you will use the **mailx** command instead of the **mail** command. Remember, you were warned earlier in this chapter that the specific **mail** command you use will depend on your version of UNIX. With **mailx**, you can start an electronic-mail message and then use the text editor **vi** (the default, anyway—your system administrator may have configured your system differently) when you want to create the text of the message. In this case, the *-v* must be on its own line, as in the following command line:

```
% mailx kreichard@mcimail.com
-v
```

After using **vi** to edit the message, you'll exit **vi** with the **ZZ** (**Save** and **Exit**) command. You'll be back in the **mailx** command; type a period (**.**) on its own line to end the input and send the message.

▲ **L E A R N   M O R E   A B O U T** ▲

Again, these commands and procedures will be covered in more detail in the next chapter.

Those using System V Release 4—the most recent version of UNIX—can attach binary files, such as programs and data files, to mail messages with the *-m* option:

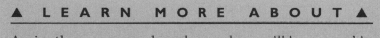

$ mail -m *datafile* kreichard@mcimail.com

where **datafile** is the name of the binary file.

Remote Access with Ftp

Depending on your version of UNIX and your system setup, you may have full access to the Internet, which allows you to communicate directly with any other Internet-connected computer in the world. (Your system administrator should be able to tell you if you have this capability.) The beauty is that the actual mechanisms for connecting to this remote computer are completely transparent to you, the user; all you need to do is know the remote address, and off you go.

The biggest plus to this is the ability to move files from a remote computer to your computer. In computer parlance, this is called *downloading* a file. To do so, you'll use two UNIX commands: **ftp** and **telnet**.

▼

The **ftp** command connects you to any other computer on the Internet. These computers may or not be using the UNIX operating system, but from your viewpoint it really doesn't matter. What's important is that both machines can use the **ftp** command.

Ftp stands for *file transfer protocol*. It is *interactive* software, which means it asks you for information at specific times. To run **ftp**, you type it on a command line:

```
$ ftp
ftp>
```

As does the **mail** command, the **ftp** command features its own prompt, letting you know that it is in charge of the computing session. To get a list of available commands, use a question mark (?) at an **ftp** prompt:

```
$ ftp> ?
```

You can also establish a direct connection to a machine either by specifying the machine's name when you begin an **ftp** session:

```
$ ftp machinename
```

or by using the **open** command after starting an **ftp** session:

```
ftp> open
(to) machinename
Connected to machinename
```

where *machinename* refers to the remote Internet-connected computer.

Reality Check: Looking for Files on the Internet

How do you know what machines to look for when you're in search for files on the Internet? Unfortunately, at this moment, the Internet is stuck in a conundrum: To look for something, you first need to know what you're looking for and where it's located. It's like trying to find a book in the library, except that the books have no information on the spines, and the card catalog isn't organized in any order.

While this situation is changing, the fact remains that you're going to get an idea of what you can get on the Internet through Usenet messages (where someone else will refer to a machine on the Internet containing specific files) or by one of the many Internet books on the market.

▼

Anonymous ftp

Under most circumstances, you need an account set up on a remote machine when you use the **ftp** command. This is especially true when you deal with the commercial world. Since it's impractical to set up an account for every user in a high-traffic situation, the practice of *anonymous ftp* evolved. Instead of having an account on the remote machine, you can login the remote machine as **anonymous**. Your privileges on the machine are extremely limited—you're allowed mainly to upload and download files from a specific directory, and that's about it—but this setup works very well.

To use anonymous **ftp**, you'd initiate an **ftp** session in the normal way. The difference is that you'd enter *anonymous* as your name, with your electronic-mail address (referred to as your *Ident*) as your password:

```
ftp> open
(to) kevin.kevinmn.com
Connected to kevin.kevinmn.com
Name (kevin.kevinmn.com): anonymous
220 Guest login ok, send ident as password.
Password: kreichard@mcimail.com
230 Guest login ok, access restrictions apply.
```

From there, you'd use the regular **ftp** commands.

Let's say you know through various sources that a really cool UNIX game is stored on the machine named *kevin.kevinmn.com* (no, this isn't a real machine) in the directory named **/games**. You also know that the name of the file is **deathrow.Z**. You would then use the following command line to connect to the machine named *kevin.kevinmn.com*:

```
$ ftp kevin.kevinmn.com
```

If the connection goes through, you'll get a message saying so, along with a login prompt. Enter *anonymous* as your name:

```
Name (kevin.kevinmn.com): anonymous
```

and then enter your full username as the password:

```
220 Guest login ok, send ident as password.
Password: kreichard@mcimail.com
```

From there, you can use the remote machine as if you were using the UNIX box in your own company. To make sure that the file you want is present, you can use the **ls** command as you would if you were looking for information on your own system. You can use **cd** to maneuver through a directory structure like the structure on your own UNIX system (that is, directories and subdirectories). In addition, you'll have access to additional **ftp** commands, as listed in Table 5.7.

Take Your time

Don't worry about doing damage when you're logged on the remote computer; you can't do any harm, and the remote system is set up so that you can't accidentally erase any important files.

TABLE 5.7 COMMAND REFERENCE FOR THE FTP COMMAND

COMMAND	PURPOSE
? *command*	Displays help for specified *command*.
ascii	Sets transfer mode to ASCII (text) format.
bell	Creates a sound (usually a beep) after a file is transferred.
binary	Sets transfer mode to binary format.
bye or **quit**	Ends ftp session and ends the **ftp** program.
cdup	Changes the current directory to one level up on the directory hierarchy; same as **cd**.
close	Ends **ftp** session with the remote machine, but continues the ftp command on the local machine.
delete *filename*	Removes *filename* from remote directory.

dir *directory filename*	Returns the contents of the specified directory; resulting information is stored in *filename*.
disconnect	Ends ftp session and **ftp** program.
get *file1 file2* or	Gets *file1* from the remote machine and stores it under.
recv *file1 file2*	the filename *file2*; if *file2* is not specified, the *file1* name will be retained.
help *command*	Displays information about specified command; displays general help information if no command is specified.
mdelete *filename(s)*	Deletes *filename(s)* on the remote machine.
mdir *filename(s)*	Returns directory for multiple, specified *filename(s)*.
mget *filename(s)*	Gets the specified multiple *filename(s)* from the remote machine.
mput *filename(s)*	Puts the specified filename(s) on the remote machine.
open *remote_machine*	Opens a connection to the specified remote machine; if no remote machine is specified, the system will prompt you for a machine name.
put *file1 file2* or **send** *file1 file3*	Puts local file *file1* on the remote machine, under the new filename *file2*; if *file2* is not specified, the file will remain with the name *file1*.
rename *file1 file2*	Renames *file1* on the remote system to the new *file2*.
rmdir *directory*	Removes *directory* from the remote machine.

▼

By looking at the contents of the current directory, you know that **deathrow.Z** is in the current directory.

Most anonymous ftp sites are set up so that the most popular files are immediately accessible, without the need to search through directories and subdirectories.

Before you do so, you need to make sure that the **ftp** command is prepared to transfer a file like this.

The *.Z* tells us that the file in question is a **compressed** file. Very often, larger files will be compressed so that the time needed to transfer them is minimized. How do you know that files are compressed? They end either with **.Z** or **.z**.

UNIX files are compressed with two different commands: **compress** and **pack**. Files compressed with the **compress** command end with **.Z**, while files compressed with the **pack** command end with **.z**.

The commands to uncompress these files will depend on the command used to compress the files. To uncompress files compressed with the **compress** command (that is, ending with **.Z**), use the **uncompress** command. In order to uncompress files compressed with the **pack** command (that is, ending with **.z**), use the **unpack** command.

Tables 5.8 and 5.9 summarize the uncompress and the **unpack** commands, respectively.

▼

▼

TABLE 5.8 COMMAND REFERENCE FOR THE UNCOMPRESS COMMAND

uncompress *option file(s)*

PURPOSE

The **uncompress** command does exactly what the name says: uncompresses a compressed file. These files usually have a name ending in **.Z**. When used, the newly compressed files will replace the original compressed file.

OPTION

-c   Uncompress without changing original *file(s)*.

TABLE 5.9 COMMAND REFERENCE FOR THE UNPACK COMMAND

unpack *file(s)*

PURPOSE

The **unpack** command unpacks a file shrunk with the **pack** commands. These files usually end with **.z**.

OPTIONS

None.

Anyway, to get to the reason for explaining compressed files. If a file is compressed, you must make sure the **ftp** command knows this. Since the compressed file is a binary file, you must tell the **ftp** command so with the following command:

```
ftp> binary
```

▼

Once you've done that, you can grab the **deathrow.Z** file with the following command:

```
ftp> get deathrow.Z
```

When the file is transferring, there's no prompt, and the system won't accept your keystrokes. After the file has been transferred to your system, the system will tell you so in this manner:

```
Transfer complete
```

When you're done transferring files, use **bye** or **quit** to end the **ftp** command:

```
ftp> bye
```

This Chapter in Review

▲ A prime reason for using the UNIX operating system is its ability to interconnect with other computer systems, as well as connect many users on one system.

▲ To communicate directly with other users on your system, use the **who** command to find out who is logged on the system, and then use the **write** or **talk** command to directly communicate with that user.

▲ UNIX also features many tools for sending and receiving electronic mail, including programs like **mail**, **mailx**, **mush**, and **elm**. They all work similarly: They allow you to read and write messages, as well as manage your mail messages.

▲ The **mail** command also allows you to send electronic mail. You can type the message directly into the system, or else you can use a text editor like **vi** to compose the message.

▲ UNIX also contains many tools that allow you to communicate with others via the Internet, a large collection of computers. These tools include newsreaders and commands for downloading files from a remote computer.

▼

▲   The **ftp** command allows you to communicate directly with other computers on the Internet to download files. When you use this command, it presents its own prompt and supports its own commands.

▲   Many files on the Internet are compressed, so they transfer quicker. To uncompress a compressed file, use the **uncompress** or **unpack** commands.

Not tonight Murray, I'm moving text.

▪ CHAPTER SIX ▪
Text Editing, Processing, and Printing

E diting text is one of the most important tools you have at your disposal. Many UNIX functions—configuration files, electronic mail,
data storage—center around text files. This chapter covers some of UNIX's
text-editing tools, including:

- ▲ Using **vi**, the Visual Editor.
- ▲ Learning the difference between **vi**'s command and insert modes.
- ▲ Editing existing text through yanking and pasting characters.
- ▲ Using the optional **emacs** text editor.
- ▲ Entering commands in **emacs**.
- ▲ Searching and replacing text within emacs.
- ▲ Saving files in both **vi** and **emacs**.
- ▲ Checking word spellings in a file with the **spell** command.
- ▲ Counting the number of words and lines in a file with the **wc** command.
- ▲ Printing files with the **lp** command.
- ▲ Tracking print requests with the **lpstat** command.
- ▲ Processing and formatting text with the **troff** command.

In many ways, this chapter represents a crossroads in your UNIX education, as it starts to wrap up some loose ends that have been hanging from the first five chapters of this book. Throughout it all, there have been repeated references to text editors and when you should use them—like creating electronic-mail messages in the manner discussed in Chapter 5.

This chapter covers the basic UNIX text editors, and specifically the two most popular text editors: **vi** and **emacs**. There are several other UNIX editors available—ranging from the relatively crude **ed** to the serviceable **xedit** (found on systems featuring the X Window System)—but by and large **vi** and **emacs** will be the editor of choice for most UNIX users.

However, be warned that **emacs** is not available on every system. **Vi** is a core portion of the UNIX operating system and is included with virtually every version of UNIX on the market. Conversely, **emacs** does not ship with most UNIX systems and must be installed separately (which is something best discussed with your system administrator).

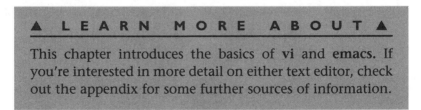

▲ L E A R N   M O R E   A B O U T ▲

This chapter introduces the basics of **vi** and **emacs**. If you're interested in more detail on either text editor, check out the appendix for some further sources of information.

Vi: The Visual Editor

Vi stands for *visual editor*, and it's used to create and edit ASCII files. Many important UNIX files are ASCII—that is, text-only files—and are therefore editable with **vi**.

When it comes to **vi**, ignorance is definitely bliss. If you've used MS-DOS or Macintosh computers, you know that these systems feature some very usable text editors—even the lowly DOS **EDIT** command is more functional than **vi**. However, if you're a truly beginning computer user, you'll probably be quite happy with **vi**, since you won't know any better.

Indeed, **vi** presents a series of plusses and minuses for you. On the plus side, **vi** is a pretty snappy performer when scrolling through long documents. It allows you to view the files one screen at a time. And it performs many of the basic functions you'd expect from a very basic text editor, albeit in a very convoluted fashion.

On the minus side, **vi** doesn't allow you to format text (such as bold or italics), and it works in a rather awkward manner—which you'll see as you run through a short **vi** session.

Starting Vi

There are two ways to start **vi**: Either with or without a file loaded. To start **vi** without a file, use the following command line:

`$ vi`

To start **vi** with a file loaded, use the following command line:

`$ vi file`

where *file* is the name of the file to be loaded or created.

When you start **vi** without a file loaded, you'll be presented with a mostly blank screen, with a cursor on the upper-left corner and a set of tilde (~) characters running down the left side of the screen, and a prompt at the bottom of the screen. The tilde characters tell you that there are no characters on the lines they head. (Remember—the space generated by the space bar isn't marked with a character on the screen.) The prompt—which isn't demarcated with a colon, by the way— is where you can enter commands, like saving files and quitting **vi**.

The many commands available when working within **vi** are listed in Table 6.1.

TABLE 6.1 COMMAND REFERENCE FOR THE VI COMMAND

vi *options file(s)*

PURPOSE
The **vi** command launches a full-screen text editor.

OPTIONS

-c *command*	Starts **vi** and runs *command*.
-C	Edit an encrypted file, which is a text file that has been changed for security reasons.
-L	Lists the files that were saved despite a system failure.
-r*file*	Recovers *file* after a system crash
-R	Run in read-only mode, which means that files cannot be changed.
-w*n*	Sets window size to *n* lines of text.
-x	Creates an encrypted file, which prevents others from reading the file.
+	Starts **vi** on the last line of the file.
+*line*	Starts **vi** with *line* as the top line in the window.

VI COMMANDS

/string	Searches for *string*, going forward.
/string	Searches for *string*, going backward.
*n*G	Goes to line number *n*.
h	Same as the **Left Arrow** key. Useful for keyboards lacking arrow keys.
j	Same as the **Down Arrow** key. Useful for keyboards lacking arrow keys.

k	Same as the **Up Arrow** key. Useful for keyboards lacking arrow keys.
l	Same as the **Right Arrow** key. Useful for keyboards lacking arrow keys.
Ctrl-F	Goes forward one page.
Ctrl-B	Goes backward one page.
ZZ	Saves file and exits.
:w	Saves file.
:q	Quits without saving file.
:wq	Saves file and quits the command.
:n	Goes to next file on the command line.
:n!	Goes to next file on the command line, even if you haven't saved the current file.
:q!	Quits without saving file.
dw	Delete word.
dd	Delete line.
i	Enter insert mode.
a	Enter append mode, inserting after current position.

At this point, you can't actually start typing away. This is because of a quirk within **vi**, which you'll have to immediately deal with—modes.

Modes Under Vi

When working with **vi**, there's one key fact to always remember: You must work in either *insert* or *command* modes. With insert mode, you can type characters. With command mode, you can enter commands.

The **vi** default is to work in command mode when you start it. This means that anything you type is interpreted by **vi** as being a command.

▼

The absurdity of this situation should be apparent—commands at this stage are rather meaningless if you've not entered any text. But **vi** doesn't tell you explicitly that you're in command mode, unless you consider a cursor on the bottom of the screen a clear indication. If you're not familiar with **vi**, you'll end up generating a series of annoying beeps when you first try to enter text.

Conversely, you can enter text when you're in insert mode. To get there from command mode, type **i**. The cursor will appear on the top-left corner of the screen, at the beginning of the ostensible document. At this point, you can go ahead and type away.

As you type, you'll notice that **vi** will just keep on inserting text at what appears to be the end of the screen. As a text editor, **vi** knows nothing about page layouts and printers; it only knows that it can accept your keystrokes, and that lines are whatever length you specify. To end a line and go to the next line, hit the **Enter** or **Return** key. The cursor keys (if your keyboard sports any, that is) can be used to navigate throughout the screen.

When you're finished entering text, you'll want to switch back to command mode, which is done by pressing the **Esc** key.

The **Esc** key is also convenient for letting you know what mode you're in—if you're not sure, just go ahead and hit the **Esc** a few times. The worst that happens is that the system beeps at you.

Even better, you can tell **vi** to tell *you* what mode it's in. To do so, go to command mode by pressing the **Esc** key and then type the following:

```
:set smd
```

This command displays *INSERT MODE* on the bottom of the screen when you are actually working in insert mode.

The commands available in command mode have to do mainly with some minimal editing tools and the saving of files. The more popular command-mode options are listed in Table 6.2.

Vi is a quirky little beast. There's no rhyme or reason to the commands. Some are straight keystrokes, some are preceded by slashes, and some are preceded with colons. At the beginning of your **vi** usage, you may want to keep a list of commands very close to your terminal, since there's no way you're going to actually remember them.

TABLE 6.2 VI COMMAND-MODE OPTIONS

COMMAND	RESULT
a	Append new characters to the right of the last position of the cursor in insert mode.
A	Append new characters to the end of the last line where the cursor was positioned in insert mode.
Esc key	Switches from insert mode to command mode.
Enter key	Moves the cursor from the end of the current line to the beginning of the following line.
i	Switches to insert mode and places the cursor at the top-left of the screen.
I	Switches to insert mode and places the cursor at the beginning of the current line.
o	Inserts new line after the last line where the cursor was positioned in insert mode.
O	Inserts new line before the last line where the cursor was positioned in insert mode.
:set smd	Informs you when **vi** is in insert mode.
/string	Searches forward through the file for the first instance of *string*.
?string	Searches backward through the file for the first instance of *string*.
x	Delete the character to the right of the cursor.
X	Delete the character to the left of the cursor.

Any of the commands listed in Table 6.2—as well as throughout this section on **vi**—can be extended by adding a numeral to the command. To delete three characters, for instance, you can type **x3**.

Editing Your Text

There's a *lot* to unlearn when using **vi**. For instance, every other text editor under the sum allows you to move the cursor over a character and then type a new character over it. In this fashion, changing *a* to *A* would be a matter of moving the cursor over the a and then typing **A**.

This is not the case with **vi**. Indeed, there are three rather convoluted methods to editing with **vi**.

Editing Method 1

This involves a deletion of the current character and then an insertion of the new character. If the cursor is *before* the character to be deleted, type **Esc** (which brings you to command mode) and then type **x**. If the cursor is *after* the character to be deleted, type **Esc** (which brings you to command mode) and then type **X**. (Remember—case counts.) After you return to insert mode by typing **i**, you can then insert the new character.

Editing Method 2

Vi features many deletion commands (as listed in Table 6.3), which you can use to both delete and insert a character. In this case, you'll want to use the **r** command to replace the character in conjunction with the character you want to replace it with. To change an *a* to an *A* in this manner, you'd switch to command mode by pressing the **Esc** key and then by typing the following:

rA

Editing Method 3

The tilde character (~), when used in command mode, changes the case of the character to the right of the cursor. To change an existing *a* to *A* (or an existing *A* to *a*), go to command mode by pressing the **Esc** key and then pressing the tilde (~) character.

The three editing methods—as well as some convenient tools for deleting text—can be found in Table 6.3.

TABLE 6.3 VI DELETION AND EDITING COMMANDS

COMMAND	RESULT
~	Changes the case of the character to the right of the cursor.
dd	Deletes the current line.
D	Deletes all characters from the cursor to the end of the line.
:D	Deletes the current line.
:D$	Deletes all characters from the cursor to the end of the line.
r*n*	Deletes the character to the right of the cursor and then inserts character *n*.
:U	Undoes the last deletion.
x	Deletes the character to the right of the cursor.

Saving a File

Saving a file should be done like voting in Chicago: early and often. While you don't need to worry too much about problems with the UNIX operating system that could wipe out your work, you still should store your work often, if only to protect yourself from yourself.

To save a file under **vi**, go to command mode by typing the **Esc** key and then type the following:

`:w filename`

where *filename* is the name you bestow on your work. The file is saved, but it still appears on your screen, so you can continue your work.

In order to save a file and then quit **vi**, use the following command line:

`ZZ`

In this situation, you would have already saved the file and given it a filename. Don't be mislead by the fact that your file is still displayed on the screen. When it quits, **vi** doesn't clear the screen. However, your prompt will appear at the bottom of the screen, telling you that the shell is open for your command.

There are other ways to store files, as listed in Table 6.4.

TABLE 6.4 VI COMMANDS FOR STORING FILES

COMMAND	RESULT
:q	**Vi** quits after the file is saved, as long as the file has been previously saved; if the file has never been saved, **vi** will refuse to quit.
:q!	**Vi** quits without storing the file.
:w	The file is saved; if it lacks a filename, **vi** will ask you for one.
:w *filename*	The file is saved under the filename *filename*.
:wq	**Vi** quits after the file is saved.
:x	**Vi** quits after the file is saved.
ZZ	**Vi** quits after the file is saved.

▼

Cutting and Pasting Text

Believe it or not, **vi** has some very rudimentary cut-and-paste capabilities. It involves yanking text and then placing the text elsewhere on the screen. The two steps are quite simple:

▲   Position the cursor at the beginning of the text you want to move, then press the **Esc** key and enter the following in command mode:

yw

which is the option for yanking a word. (Other yanking options are listed in Table 6.3.)

▲   Move the cursor to the spot where you want to insert the text. To paste the yank to the *right* of the cursor, type:

p

followed by the **Return** key. To paste the yank to the *left* of the cursor, type:

P

There's a lot more to **vi** than is presented in this somewhat sardonic chapter. Indeed, whole books have been written about **vi**. If you're really interested in getting as much as possible out of **vi**, check out the appendix for a list of recommended works.

Emacs: A More Modern Editor

As you'll recall from the beginning of this chapter, **emacs** is not featured on every UNIX system. It's a product of the Free Software Foundation, which encourages its use by giving it away essentially. In this case, the old adage "you don't get what you pay for" certainly does not apply—you get a lot more in the case of **emacs**.

If your system setup allows it, you should install **emacs** on your system or request that your system administrator do so for you.

▼

Emacs is an example of what is called *freeware*. There's a ton of UNIX freeware on the market.

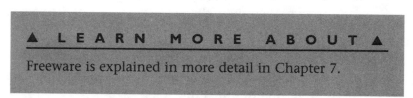

▲ L E A R N   M O R E   A B O U T ▲

Freeware is explained in more detail in Chapter 7.

In this chapter, we'll assume you or someone else has already installed **emacs** on your system. Though there are many versions of **emacs** floating around, the procedures presented here should apply pretty much to any version of **emacs**.

This is Technical

If you're not yet comfortable with basic UNIX usage, you may want to avoid using **emacs** for the time being. **Emacs** can be a challenging program for the neophyte. Also, note that there are *a ton* of advanced features to **emacs** that will be totally ignored in this chapter.

Starting Emacs

There are two ways to start **emacs**—either without a file loaded:

emacs

or with a file loaded:

emacs *filename*

where *filename* is the name of the file you want loaded.

When you start **emacs** without a file loaded, you'll be presented with a mostly blank screen with a status bar on the bottom, indicating the name of the file you're working on, the size of the file, and your position in the file.

You'll immediately note that **emacs** is on one level easier to use than **vi**: There's only one mode at all times, as opposed to **vi**'s command and insert modes. Therefore, you can go ahead and enter text directly from the get-go. Like **vi**, however, you'll have to press **Enter** or **Return** at the end of every line.

The Meta Key

One of the more evil aspects of the UNIX operating system—especially for beginners—is its use of a *Meta* key.

Since no one controls UNIX, there's never been one central authority to make sure that UNIX was implemented uniformly across offerings from different vendors. In UNIX's history, each vendor approached UNIX a little differently, both in terms of software implementations and in terms of hardware. A computer running UNIX from Hewlett-Packard, for example, would feature a monitor and keyboard different than a computer running UNIX from Sun Microsystems. (Indeed, different UNIX computers from Sun would feature a range of keyboards themselves.)

However, it was clear that there was a need for additional modifier keys when it came to commands. Thus were born *modifier keys* like the **Ctrl** key and the **Alt** key. But since not every UNIX hardware vendor included **Ctrl** and **Alt** keys on their systems, UNIX designers couldn't assume that the same keys were present on every UNIX keyboard.

The solution was the **Meta** key, which would vary depending on the vendor and the keyboard layout. On PC-style keyboards (which, thankfully, are becoming more prevalent in the UNIX marketplace), the **Meta** key is usually labeled **Alt**. On older Sun SPARCstation keyboards, the **Meta** key has a diamond shape on it and is located next to the space bar; it is not the key marked **Alt**. On other older Sun keyboards, the **Meta** keys are labeled **Left** and **Right**. On some Hewlett-Packard systems, the **Meta** key is labeled **Extend Char**.

The lesson: Check with your system administrator to see what key you should use on your system. If there's an **Alt** key on your keyboard, chances are pretty good that you should be using this key when you see a reference to **Meta** in this section. (If this doesn't work, try using the **Esc** key.)

Accessing Emacs Commands Via the Keyboard

Why is this important? Because most important **emacs** commands are entered directly from the keyboard in conjunction with the **Ctrl** and **Meta** keys.

For example, **Ctrl-** and **Meta**-key combinations allow you to move around the screen—a throwback to the days when UNIX keyboards didn't feature cursor keys. (However, if your keypad features a cursor keypad and keys like **PageUp** and **PageDn**, these should work.)

The handier cursor commands are listed in Table 6.5.

TABLE 6.5 HANDY EMACS CURSOR KEYBOARD COMMANDS

COMMAND	RESULT
Ctrl-L	Moves the current cursor line to the middle of the screen.
Ctrl-V	Moves the document forward one screen.
Meta-V	Moves the document backward one screen.
Meta-<	Places the beginning of the document at the top of the screen.
Meta->	Places the end of the document at the bottom of the screen.

Searching and Replacing Text

Emacs allows you to search for a specific set of characters and replace them with another set of characters. To do so, begin by typing **Ctrl-S**, which will summon a prompt on the bottom of the screen:

Search for:

or

I-search:

At this point, you'll enter the desired characters, making sure that they are the same case as the characters you're searching for. When you're through, press **Enter**.

To search backward through a file, use **Ctrl-R** instead of **Ctrl-S**.

Deleting Characters and Lines

If your keyboard features **Backspace (BkSp)** or **Delete (Del)** keys, you can use them to delete characters with **emacs**. Other **emacs** deletion commands are listed in Table 6.6.

TABLE 6.6 EMACS DELETION COMMANDS

COMMAND	RESULT
Ctrl-K	Deletes all characters through the end of the line.
Meta-D	Deletes to the beginning of the next word.
Meta-Del	Deletes backward to the beginning of the previous word.

Saving Your Work

As always, save early and save often. To save a file with **emacs**, type **Ctrl-x** and then **Ctrl-s**. At this point, **emacs** will ask you for the name of the file if it lacks a name.

▼

If you want to save your file and quit **emacs** in one step, type **Ctrl-x** and then **Ctrl-c**.

Cutting and Pasting Text

You'll find that **emacs** is also more advanced than **vi** when it comes to cutting and pasting text. As opposed to **vi**'s practice of yanking a single character and then moving it elsewhere, **emacs** allows you to move an entire section of text.

The steps for moving text are simple:

1. Mark the text.
2. Cut the text.
3. Move the cursor to the point where you want to place the text.
4. Paste the text.

In order to mark the text, move your cursor to the beginning of the text you want to move and then press **Ctrl-@**. From there, move your cursor to the end of the text you want to move and then type **Ctrl-w**. The "marked" text disappears. (Unfortunately, **emacs** doesn't physically mark the text that you want to move; you'll have to rely on your memory.)

This is technical

When you run **emacs**, you're also setting aside some system memory for a *kill buffer*. When you move text, you're really moving it to the kill buffer, and from there you're pasting it to the new location.

Take
Your
time

You don't need to worry at all about setting up or maintaining a kill buffer. Don't worry that your text actually disappears—it's merely being moved to another part of the system.

▼

Now move the cursor to the point on the screen where you want to paste the deleted text. When you do this, type **Ctrl-y**. This summons the deleted text from the kill buffer.

When in Doubt, Yell for Help

Help systems are a rarity in the UNIX world. Too often, UNIX programmers are too harried and hurried to put good help systems in their software. (Indeed, you're more than halfway through a UNIX text and you've not been told *once* about the existence of any online help.)

To summon **emacs**'s online help, use one of the following commands: **Ctrl-H**, the **F1** key, **Esc-?**, **Meta-?**, or **Meta-x**. There's no way to predict which one of these combinations will actually bring up the help system, although **Ctrl-H** is usually a good bet.

Using Other Text-Related Commands

Though **vi** and **emacs** are the two most popular text editors, there are a number of text-related commands you'll find useful.

The Spell Command

The UNIX command **spell** will check the spelling in a text file against a database of words contained in another file.

If a word in a text file doesn't appear in the database, the **spell** command will return the word.

To run *spell* on a file, use the following command line:

```
$ spell filename
```

where *filename* is the name of the file to check. Depending on the specific misspelled words, of course, the output will look something like:

```
$ spell filename
Taht
spel
depnds
relevent
$
```

In this case, there are only a few misspelled words. How-ever, if you're using the **spell** command on a larger file, you'll probably generate many more misspellings, so you'll want to redirect the output of the command to a file:

```
$ spell file > errors
```

To view this file, use the **cat** command:

```
$ cat errors
```

 The **spell** command really doesn't check spellings. Instead, it matches the words in your files against a master file that is not the most complete database available. There will be many words that are spelled correctly and returned by **spell** as being spelled incorrectly because they don't appear in the **spell** database. Also, because **spell** doesn't really check for spellings, this command will not suggest correct spellings to "misspelled" words.

The **spell** command is summarized in Table 6.7.

TABLE 6.7 COMMAND REFERENCE FOR THE SPELL COMMAND

spell *options files*

PURPOSE

The **spell** command lists "incorrectly" spelled words—that is, words not contained in a file of correctly spelled words—in a file.

OPTIONS

-b	Checks for spellings based on British usage.
+*filename*	Creates a sorted file (*filename*) of correctly spelled words.

Using the Wc Command

The **wc** command does one thing: It counts the number of words in a file, as in the following command line.

For example, the following **wc** command output lists the number of lines (10), words (55), characters (332), and the filename (file):

```
$ wc file
10 55    332 file
```

The **wc** command is summarized in Table 6.8.

TABLE 6.8 COMMAND REFERENCE FOR THE WC COMMAND

wc *options file(s)*

PURPOSE

The **wc** command counts the number of words, characters, and lines in a text file.

OPTIONS

-c   Print only the number of characters.

-l   Print only the number of lines.

-w   Print only the number of words.

Printing Files

Once you create a text file in **vi** or **emacs** and check its spelling with **spell**, you'll naturally want to print it. This is a simple matter of using the **lp** command, which is summarized in Table 6.9.

Some UNIX systems use the **lpr** command instead of the **lp** command. However, the command lines as used in this section can be used with either **lp** or **lpr**—for the most part, anyway, since there's a wide variance in the **lp** command from system to system, and not every option is featured on every system. Check with your system administrator to see what print command your particular system uses and what options are supported.

TABLE 6.9 COMMAND REFERENCE FOR THE LP COMMAND

lp *options files*

PURPOSE

The **lp** command sends a print request to a printer, consisting of a single file or multiple files.

OPTIONS

-c	Copies the file to a print spooler before sending the request.	
-d *printer*	Specifies a printer other than the default printer.	
-H *action*	Prints according to one of these actions:	
	hold	Suspends current or pending print job.
	immediate	Prints immediately after current job is completed.
	resume	Resumes suspended print job.
-m	Sends a mail message to the user when the file is printed.	
-n *num*	Prints *num* number of copies (the default is 1).	
-o *option*	Sets printer-specific options:	
	cpi=*n*	Prints *n* characters per inch; **pica**, **elite**, or **compressed** can be used instead of *n*.
	length=*n*	Page length, specified in inches (*ni*), lines (*n*), or centimeters (*nc*).
	lpi=*n*	Prints *n* lines per inch.

nobanner	Do not print the banner page.
nofilebreak	Do not print form feed between files.
stty=*list*	Returns a *list* of options for **stty.**
width=*n*	Page width, specified in inches (*n*i), lines (*n*), or centimeters (*n*c).
-P *list*	Prints the page numbers specified by *list*.
-t *title*	Prints *title* banner on every page.
-w	Sends a terminal message to the user when the file is printed.

For example, to print a file named **letter**, you'd use the following command line:

```
$ lp letter
UX: lp: request id is hplaser-211 (1 file)
$
```

The **lp** command tells you that the file is being printed on the printer named *hplaser* and has an ID of 211.

This is Technical

Printing files under UNIX can be complicated—at least when it comes to setting up printers. This is a task best left to system administrators. For the purposes of this section, we'll assume that the printer is properly configured. In regard to your specific printer situation, check with your system administrator.

In the previous example, your file was printed on a printer named *hplaser*. There may be many printers on a larger UNIX network, however, so you have the option of choosing another printer on which to print your file. Your system administrator keeps a list of installed printers— or if not, should—for your use. To use another printer on the network, you'll need to know its name (or number), and then name it on a command line, along with the -*d* option. The following command line prints the file **letter** to a printer named *laser*:

```
$ lp -d laser letter
UX: lp: request id is laser-211 (1 file)
$
```

▼

When you print a file, you're actually sending the request to another UNIX file, which keeps track of all print requests and makes sure that they are printed in the order they are entered into the system. The system will actually print the file when it's good and ready. However, as you're working on a file there may be times when you give the command to print the file, and then make changes to the file. Since you can't predict exactly when the system prints the file, there's the chance that the system will print the file after you make the changes. To avoid this, you may want to always print files with the use of the *-c* option, which uses the original file for printing:

```
$ lp -c letter
UX: lp: request id is hplaser-211 (1 file)
$
```

After this, you can go ahead and make changes to the **letter** file; they won't appear in what you print.

Canceling Print Requests

When you use the **lp** command, you'll notice that the system assigned an ID to the request. You can use this information to cancel the print request, should you change your mind or discover that another user has sent a *monster* 500-page document to the printer, thus keeping it occupied for a while.

The following command line will cancel the print request made in the previous section:

```
$ cancel hplaser-211
request "hplaser-211" canceled
$
```

If you don't remember the ID of the print request, you can use the **lpstat** command to generate a list of print requests. Actually, you may have many occasions to use this command. This command, for instance, would inform you that another user is printing a monster 400-page document, so that you shouldn't be rushing to the printer and waiting for your little letter to appear.

You can use the **lpstat** command with no options:

```
$ lpstat
hp-112 kevin 1123 May 1 11:29 on hp
hp-199 geisha 1000009 May 1 11:32
```

In this case, you can see the ID numbers for two print requests (112 and 199), that *kevin* and *geisha* sent files for printing, the size of the files in bytes (*kevin*'s modest 1123-byte file versus *geisha*'s massive 1000009-byte file), the time the print request was made (in this case, *kevin* was lucky to get his request in before *geisha*'s monster request), and the status of the request (the actual printing of which is marked with the *on* notation).

Options to the **lpstat** command are listed in Table 6.10.

TABLE 6.10 COMMAND REFERENCE FOR THE LPSTAT COMMAND

lpstat *options*

PURPOSE

The **lpstat** command lists the status of print requests, either individually or systemwide.

OPTIONS

-d	Shows the name of the default destination printer.
-r	Shows whether the print scheduler (or print spooler, as controlled by the **lpsched** command) is on or off.
-R	Shows the position of a job in the queue.
-s	Summarizes print status.
-t	Shows all status information.

Text Processing

UNIX also features a slew of commands that are used to format text: **troff**, **nroff**, and **ditroff**. While these commands should generally be used by advanced users, it's good to explain exactly how these commands work. In this section, we'll use **troff** as an example, although the concepts apply equally well to **nroff** or **ditroff**.

Troff is a UNIX *filter*. You don't use this command directly. Instead, you use a text file as input for **troff**, which then uses commands embedded within the text as formatting commands.

For instance, you can use a text file created in **vi** or **emacs** as input for **troff**. When you create the files, however, you must insert **troff** formatting commands. Most of these commands begin with a period (.) or a backslash (\).

A list of these commands is contained in Table 6.11.

TABLE 6.11 USEFUL TROFF COMMANDS

COMMAND	RESULT
.ad	Turns off line justification.
.bp	Inserts a line break, which ends one page and begins a new page.
.ce	Centers the following line of text.
.ce *n*	Centers the next *n* lines of the file.
.in *n*	Indents the following lines by *n* spaces.
.ls *n*	Specifies the line spacing.
.pl *n*	Specifies *n* number of lines on a page. The default is 66.
.po *ni*	Sets the left margin to *n* inches.
.ti *n*	Indents the first line of a paragraph by *n* spaces.

You'll notice that there's no Command Reference for the **troff** command. Why? Because it's an amazing complex command—for instance, there are **84** commands available when working within **troff**. In this instance, the most useful commands are listed in their own tables.

As mentioned, these commands must be embedded in your original text file. For instance, to center a line, your text file must look like this:

```
.ce1
This line is to be centered when printed.
```

Commands that begin with a dot (.) must be on their own line. Commands that begin with a backslash (\), which are less frequently used, can be anywhere in the text.

After you've created a file and inserted the **troff** formatting commands, you then use the command to prepare the file for printing. To display the file on the screen, use **troff** and the filename without specifying a printer:

```
$ troff testfile
```

To print the formatted file, you must specify a printer after telling **troff** that its output is indeed destined for a printer:

```
$ troff -hplaser testfile : lp
```

There's a lot more to the **troff** command than is indicated by this short introduction. In addition, there are many other tools for text formatting, such as the Memorandum Macros, that are geared for more experienced users. Check the Appendix for some further sources of information.

This Chapter in Review

▲ There are a number of text editors for UNIX users. Some, like **ed**, are extremely crude and primitive. The two most popular UNIX text editors are **vi** (which is available on virtually every UNIX system) and **emacs** (which is not available on most UNIX systems, but which can be easily added).

▲ **Vi** stands for *visual editor*, and with it you can edit text one page at a time. You work in two modes: command (where you enter commands into the system) or insert (where you can type in new text or make changes to existing text).

▲ **Emacs**, from the Free Software Foundation, is a sophisticated editor that many beginners may find disconcerting at first. However, after a little usage, beginners will realize how functional **emacs** really is—especially when compared to other UNIX text editors.

▲ Commands can be entered at any time in **emacs**. There's no reason to switch between modes to enter commands.

▲ **Emacs** also features a very functional cut-and-paste process, where you can move chunks of text from one part of the file to another part of the text.

▲ You can print files with the **lp** or **lpr** commands (the command you use will depend on your system configuration. To track your print requests, use the **lpstat** command. To cancel a print request, use the cancel command.

▲ To specify formatting within a document, use **troff** to turn embedded commands into instructions the printer can understand.

▪ CHAPTER SEVEN ▪
UNIX Freeware

The UNIX operating system can take advantage of a rich tradition of low-cost or no-cost software, called freeware. You've already seen an example of *freeware* in Chapter 4, with the discussion of **emacs**. Topics in this short chapter include:

▲   What exactly is freeware.

▲   Acquiring freeware via the Internet and CD-ROM vendors.

▲   Freeware versions of UNIX: Linux and 386BSD.

▲   Offerings from the Free Software Foundation.

Free Software

The UNIX operating system boasts a rich tradition of freeware—that is, software created by individuals and then given away for all to use. At its roots UNIX has a deep entrenchment in the university and academic worlds, where such sharing is highly encouraged and prized.

While most vendor releases of UNIX are complete in what they offer, there's always the chance that you could do better by looking around for some freeware. In the previous chapter, for instance, you were tutored on the finer points of using **emacs**, freeware from the

Free Software Foundation. Anyone serious about text editing is probably going to want to consider **emacs** at one point or another, yet virtually no UNIX vendors ship it.

How Do I Get Freeware?

Acquiring freeware can be simple, or it can be difficult. For starters, you really should talk with your system administrator if you are unhappy with any of the UNIX tools at your disposal. If you don't like **vi**, then tell your system administrator and request an alternative. It may be that your system administrator has already installed **emacs** for some users and is willing to do so for you. Or you may have a heaven-sent system administrator who's willing to go out and look for freeware.

The best place to start looking for freeware is the Internet. Aside from electronic mail, software distribution is the biggest use for the Internet. The procedures for grabbing files from the Internet were outlined in Chapter 5 (here's a chance for you to put those **ftp** skills to immediate use).

However, there's one conundrum to working with the Internet— there's still no good way to browse for software offerings. That's no problem if you want to grab the software described in this chapter— the corresponding e-mail address is listed. But keeping track of new titles is another method. Quite honestly, there's no good way to approach this problem. If you have a specific need, you can post a message to a Usenet newsgroup (see the Appendix for a list) and wait for a reply. Or you can read Richard Morin's monthly column, "The Internet Notebook," in *UNIX Review*. While the column is mostly geared toward *UNIX Review*'s advanced readership, you may be able to pick up a few nuggets here and there.

> *Subscription queries can be sent to P.O. Box 420035, Palm Coast, FL 32142-0035; it's also carried on any decent newsstand.*

Another source is CD-ROM vendors, who typically ship a ton of freeware on a disk for under $50. These vendors are growing by leaps and bounds; again, check out the ads in *UNIX Review* for a sampling.

UNIX as Freeware

Some of you may be using freeware or considering its use through one of the popular, freely available PC-based UNIX *workalikes* available. They are workalikes because they technically aren't UNIX as licensed from Novell, but for the vast majority of situations this shouldn't make a difference. And they are much cheaper than the hundreds of dollars you can expect to pay for SCO UNIX or Novell's UnixWare.

With all this in mind, what can you expect from a UNIX workalike on the PC? Well, you can expect full support of the UNIX command set. You can expect most of the standard UNIX utilities. You can expect a stable programming environment. And you don't have to give up a thing when it comes to graphics—you'll have access to the X Window System.

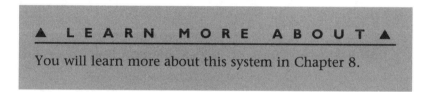

▲ L E A R N   M O R E   A B O U T ▲

You will learn more about this system in Chapter 8.

You can purchase OSF/Motif from third parties. But you can also expect minimal or even nonexistent support. And you can expect a demanding operating system that will expose every hardware flaw in your computer system.

Perhaps the leading PC UNIX workalike is Linux (pronounced *lih-nux*, according to developer Linus Torvalds), which has garnered a ton of attention among folks who are shopping for a low-cost UNIX workalike for their home computers. Linux was designed as a stripped-down UNIX clone and has been available for several years.

And, for all practical purposes, you won't know that you're not using the "real" UNIX. In fact, the following features that are available as part of Linux are also found in commercial UNIX releases:

▲ X Window System implementation through XFree86 1.3.
▲ MIME and Andrew multimedia mail.

▲ Full support of the UNIX command set.

▲ Two versions of **emacs** (which you learn about in Chapter 4).

▲ The GNU C/C++ compiler.

▲ **L E A R N   M O R E   A B O U T** ▲

You will learn more about the GNU C/C++ compiler later in this chapter.

To run Linux, you'll need at least a 386- or 486-based PC with least 2MB of RAM and a single floppy.

Because Linux takes advantage of the 386 architecture, it can't run on a 286-based PC.

This is the minimum installation, and it won't allow you to do a lot (for instance, you can't run X Window with only 2MB of RAM). More realistically, you're looking at 8–12 megabytes (MB) of RAM and a hard drive larger than 100 megabytes if you want to run X Window and a full assortment or applications. (There's no official support of the Intel Pentium chip yet, although users have reported running Linux on a Pentium-based PC with no problems.). And while you should run into no problems running the basic Linux on a vanilla clone, you can run into problems if you want to tackle higher video resolutions (handy when using X Window) and disk controllers.

FTP locations for Linux are listed in Table 7.1.

TABLE 7.1 FTP LOCATIONS FOR LINUX

SITE	DIRECTORY
ftp.funet.fi	/pub/OS/Linux
sunsite.unc.edu	/pub/Linux
tsx-11.mit.edu	/pub/linux

An alternative to Linux is a member of the 386BSD family (386BSD, FreeBSD, and Net386). These are 32-bit operating systems that claim full compliance with the BSD 4.3 version of UNIX. While there are differences between the three (the full history of this software-development process would be akin to a soap opera), your best bet—especially if you're a UNIX beginner—is FreeBSD. According to information distributed by the 386BSD development team, FreeBSD is a cleaned-up version of 386BSD, with many utilities in the system updated: "This system [FreeBSD] is not quite as leading edge as NetBSD and is intended to be used as a stable operating environment. The emphasis seems to be on better packaging and improved operation." (Does this mean that NetBSD is intended to be used as an unstable operating environment?)

The minimum hardware configuration for FreeBSD is a 386-based PC with a graphics card, 2 megabytes of RAM, and a 20-megabyte hard disk. Again, this is a minimum; a more realistic assessment would be 8 megabytes of RAM and a 100-megabyte-plus hard disk.

You can grab FreeBSD from the Internet at *FreeBSD.cdrom.com*.

The Free Software Foundation

Perhaps the most important purveyor of free software in the UNIX world today is the Free Software Foundation. Dedicated to the use of good tools that are widely distributed, the Free Software Foundation has put together an impressive list of programs and commands that run on almost any version of UNIX.

Here's a listing of the more applicable packages for the beginning UNIX user. Keep in mind that this listing represents only a small portion of what's available from the FSF.

BASH

The Bourne Again SHell (BASH) is compatible with the Bourne Shell (**sh**) and, according to the FSF, offers other features found in the C shell (**csh**) and the Korn shell (**ksh**).

GCC

This C compiler is widely used by programmers. Many UNIX vendors charge extra for a C compiler (including all of the PC UNIX vendors), so the use of the GNU C compiler is very popular in the computer world. If you're at all interested in programming, this is the cheapest way to learn about C programming with a pretty good compiler.

NetFax

Adding fax capabilities to a UNIX system can be a huge pain, as your system administrator can tell you. The FSF offers *NetFax*, a fax spooling system originally developed in the MIT Artificial Intelligence Lab. It provides Group 3 fax transmission and reception services for a networked UNIX system. It requires a Class 2 fax modem.

Assorted Utilities

The FSF offers replacement versions of many standard UNIX tools, including **ls**, **mkdir**, **mv**, **mvdir**, **rm**, and **rmdir**.

GNU Chess and GnuGo

OK, so not all of the freeware in the world is intended for serious corporate use. But *GNU Chess* is a great chess platform, pitting the wiles of the computer against your chess skills. On the other hand, the documentation for *GnuGo* clearly states that this version of Go is not yet "sophisticated."

Getting This Software

The programs listed here are available on the machine *prep.ai.mit.edu,* which you can login via anonymous FTP, in the **/pub/gnu** directory. If you use **ls** on this directory, you'll generate a very large listing. Instead, you'll want to get one of the following files, which contains more information about the FSF and its offerings: **DESCRIPTIONS, README,** and **ORDERS.**

Contacting the FSF

You can reach the Free Software Foundation at Free Software Foundation, 675 Massachusetts Av., Cambridge, MA 02139, 617/876-3296 (voice), 617/492-9057 (fax), *gnu@prep.ai.mit.edu.*

Other Free Software

Don't assume that this short chapter can even begin to introduce you to the joys of UNIX freeware. There's a lot of really good software out there. With a little effort, you can probably match your needs (as they evolve) to available software.

This Chapter in Review

▲ UNIX boasts a rich tradition of free software, called freeware.

▲ In fact, you can acquire a working version of UNIX itself as freeware.

▲ The most popular freeware versions of UNIX are Linux and the 386BSD family. Both are complete implementations of UNIX, with most of the bells and whistles you would expect from a commercial UNIX release.

▲ Acquiring UNIX freeware can be a challenge, unless you spend a lot of time poking around the Internet. All of the programs listed here can be downloaded from the Internet. In addition, many CD-ROM vendors also offer these programs on under-$50 CD-ROMs.

▲ Perhaps the most important creator and distributor of freeware in the Free Software Foundation (FSF). You were already exposed to a popular FSF offering in Chapter 4, **emacs**. Some of the other offerings of the Free Software Foundation are summarized in this chapter.

▪ CHAPTER EIGHT▪
Graphical Computing with the X Window System

A graphical interface puts a happy face on the UNIX operating system. With flashy graphics and colors, you are (in theory) capable of getting more out of your UNIX computing experience, which in turn increases your personal productivity. This chapter provides an overview to the X Window System—the most popular UNIX graphical interface— through coverage of the following topics:

▲ An overview of the graphical interface and UNIX.

▲ Learning about the X Window System and its variants, OSF/Motif and OpenWindows.

▲ Using various window managers.

▲ Learning more about the Motif Window Manager, the most popular window manager.

▲ Using the mandatory mouse.

▲ Using **xterm**, which gives you a UNIX prompt.

▲ Using **xterm** to launch other applications, like **xclock**

▲ Working with the window with focus.

▲ Using the Motif Window Manager's title bar and decorations.

▲ Using the mouse cursor to make your way around the screen.

▲ Learning to acknowledge the inevitable power of the window manager.

What is Graphical Computing?

When UNIX was young and computing was really in its infancy, UNIX users didn't even use a monitor or standard keyboard when they were computing. Instead, they used loud, clanging teletype terminals to enter UNIX commands, or (if they were truly deprived) they used punch cards to enter commands.

UNIX still owes some of its terminology to this age. For instance, the UNIX documentation will refer often to the "bell." This quite literally was a bell on the terminal, akin to the sound made by a typewriter near the end of a line. Of course, there are no bells on a UNIX system today (although there are plenty of bells and whistles); today's UNIX computers beep instead of clang, and there are monitors and keyboards instead of punch cards and Teletype terminals.

These text-based monitors use text characters to convey information one line at a time. According to various surveys, most UNIX users still use text-based terminals in the corporate world. But that is changing, as many UNIX vendors and system administrators recognize the many benefits associated with a graphical interface.

A *graphical interface* uses graphics of various sorts to convey information to you, the end user. These graphics are centered around windows, which are the domain of individual UNIX applications.

As you'll remember from the previous chapter, UNIX allows you to run multiple applications simultaneously. A graphical interface merely places them all on the screen at one time.

However, there's one thing to remember about a UNIX graphical interface: That underneath it is still good old UNIX. At any point you can run a graphical program called **xterm** and have access to your familiar UNIX prompt. Files and directories are stored the same no matter if there's a graphical interface present or not.

The most popular graphical interface in the UNIX world is the X Window system (commonly referred to as X) and the corresponding software—OSF/Motif and OpenWindows. The latter two are shown in Figure 8.1 (the Motif Window Manager) and Figure 8.2 (the Open Look Window Manager).

Figure 8.1 The Motif Window Manager

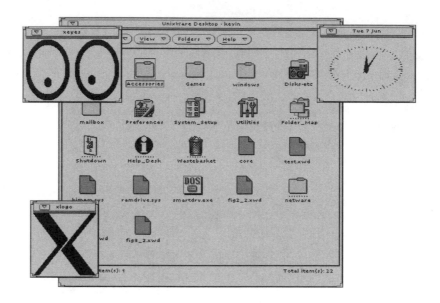

Figure 8.2 The Open Look Window Manager

X may be many things to many people, but first and foremost it allows you to open multiple windows run by multiple applications. It also allows you to take full advantage of graphics in your work. While there's much to your work doesn't require graphics—indeed, the basic tasks outlined throughout this book can be done either with a graphical interface or a character-based interface—there are many other computing tasks that can be enhanced with graphics. For instance, you can actually do professional-quality word processing with the likes of *WordPerfect for UNIX* if you have X Window installed. Similarly, software packages like *FrameMaker* (desktop publishing) and *CorelDRAW! for UNIX* (graphics) required the X Window System.

If there's one truism in the X world, it's that there's no such thing as a "typical" X installation. There are a variety of programs, called *window managers*, that affect how a window manager appears on your screen. In addition, these window managers themselves are customizable in terms of the shapes of the windows and their colors. The examples in this chapter will revolve around OSF/Motif and the Motif Window Manager (**mwm**), since it's the most popular graphical interface in the UNIX world.

Unless your UNIX system is limited to a single-user setup and you have absolute say over what goes on, the decision to go with X Window is made by the system administrator, provided your system is even capable of supporting X.

OSF/Motif

X, by itself, is pretty minimal. OSF/Motif, from the Open Software Foundation, is offered by every leading UNIX vendor and by far is the most popular interface in the UNIX world.

There are many facets to OSF/Motif, but as far as you're concerned OSF/Motif's greatest importance occurs through the Motif Window Manager, a program that sits between you and the UNIX system, interpreting your commands.

Sound familiar? It should. The window manager usurps some of the powers of the shell, which you learned about in Chapter 4.

The window manager's place in the greater scheme of things is shown in Figure 8.3.

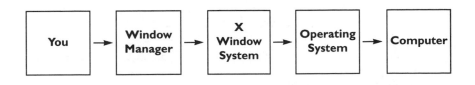

Figure 8.3 The system, the shell, the window manager, and you

▼

Using X

There are many ways to start X. Most often a UNIX system is already configured to run X and the Motif Window Manager. In these instances, you'll login and directly go into the Motif Window Manager.

This is technical

If your system is not set up to run X out of the box, check with your system administrator about setting it up to do so automatically. There are a number of ways to start X, depending on the vendor and the X implementation.

For the most part, you're not going to be using X directly. Instead, you'll be using X–based applications that not available in a character-based environment.

Using the Mouse

X Window assumes that you have a mouse on your system—and specifically a three–button mouse. However, the actions performed by these mouse buttons will depends on which window manager you use. For instance, what happens when you press the left mouse button under OSF/Motif is different than what happens when you press the left mouse button under Open Look. Check your documentation or bend your system administrator's ear to see exactly what your mouse is set up to do.

Xterm

Probably the most popular X Window application, **xterm** is a DEC VT102 terminal emulator, providing a direct window to the UNIX operating system. In it, you can enter your familiar UNIX commands like **ls**. Some

▼

X implementations are set up to automatically launch **xterm** every time X is loaded, while other users have to launch it themselves by adding a line to a file that runs every time X is started.

This is Technical

The procedure outlined next should be used only if you want to load **xterm** every time you load X. In it, you're editing a very essential file, so take care.

The file is called **.xinitrc** and is usually found in your home directory. (Not every UNIX system features this file. If you use **ls -a** to list the contents of your home directory and don't find this file, check with your system administrator for the equivalent on your system.) Use **vi**, **emacs**, or another text editor to add the following line to the file:

```
$ xterm -geom 80x40+100+200 &
```

This starts **xterm** with a window geometry of 80 characters wide and 40 lines tall, starting 100 pixels from the left-hand side of the screen and 200 pixels down from the top of the screen.

Take Your time

Window geometries will play a minor role in your computing experiences. The previous command line is presented only to show you how to open an **xterm** window in a convenient location.

When you add this line, make sure that it's not the *last* line in the file. Generally speaking, a line similar to:

```
exec mwm
```

will be the last line in the file. For X to work properly, this line must be the last line in the file.

Some users—including this author—launch three **xterms** on a window and use them for various purposes. If for no other reason, you'll find **xterm** to be handy because it keeps track of your UNIX commands, even after they apparently have scrolled off the screen. You can back up the information displayed on the screen thanks to scrollbars, which can be dragged up and down to redisplay your keystokes. Scrollbars are illustrated in Figure 8.4.

Figure 8.4 A typical xterm window

To start an **xterm** from within another **xterm** window, use the following command line:

```
$ xterm &
```

You can also use **xterm** to launch other X-based applications. The command for the X application is given in an **xterm** window, and then the new application is contained in its own window. For instance, to load a popular clock called **xclock** from **xterm**, you'd enter the following command line:

```
$ xclock &
[1] 12345
$
```

Xclock is shown in Figure 8.5.

Figure 8.5 Xclock in action

 Not every UNIX vendor ships **xterm** under that name. IBM, for instance, supports what it calls **aixterm**. Other vendors use similarly different names: Sun uses **cmdtool**, Hewlett-Packard uses **hpterm**, and Silicon Graphics uses both **xwsh** and **wsh**.

Reality Check: Problems with X

X is probably a more fragile creature than its proponents would have you believe. Because of its complexity, there's a score of things that can go wrong when you try and do some very basic things with X.

▼

For instance, there are a few error messages that you'll occasionally encounter:

Error: Cannot open display

Connection refused by server

In both of these cases, you'll need to talk with your system administrator, who has the dubious pleasure of finding out what is causing these errors and how to fix them. In fact, your system administrator should *always* be the one to fix X errors for you. Mucking around with X can be a treacherous activity indeed.

Working with the Active Window

Because X is capable of opening several windows—in other words, several applications—you'll need to know which window is capable of receiving your input.

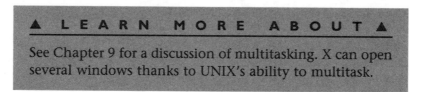

▲ L E A R N   M O R E   A B O U T ▲

See Chapter 9 for a discussion of multitasking. X can open several windows thanks to UNIX's ability to multitask.

In X, the window that can receive your input is called the window with *focus*. In the case of **mwm**, the window with focus has a different color than the other windows. If the application features a cursor, then the cursor in that window is blinking.

To change which window has the focus, position the mouse cursor anywhere over the window and then press the left mouse button.

Using the Mwm Window Manager

There are several window managers available in the X Window world. However, the most popular is the Motif Window Manager (**mwm**), which has been referred to several times in this chapter.

While using **mwm** is not especially difficult, there are some things you should be aware of when you use it.

Mwm, as well as other X Window window managers, place a *title bar* and other *decorations* around windows. The title bar tells you exactly what application is running, as the name of the application is contained within the title bar. The decorations place a number of controls around the window, which allow you to manipulate the window. The title bar and decorations are illustrated in Figure 8.7.

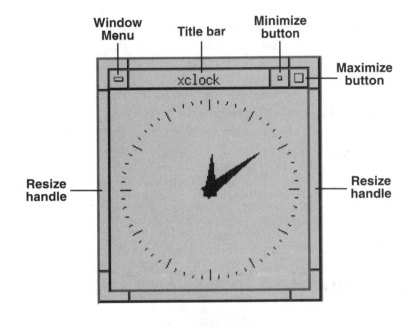

Figure 8.6 The Motif Window Manager illustrated

You use a *mouse cursor* to manipulate the objects on a screen. In **mwm**, the mouse cursor is a crosshatch. (It is different on other window managers.) You use the mouse to move the mouse cursor from one point on the window to another.

When placed over a title bar, the mouse cursor can be used to move the window. Simply place the mouse cursor over the title bar and press on the first mouse button, keeping the button depressed, and then move the mouse. You'll see that an outline of the window

▼

moves, and a little box pops up, indicating the coordinates of the screen. (Ignore the coordinates.)

The mouse cursor can be used for other routine actions. Place the mouse cursor over the Minimize button and press the left mouse button; this will cause the window to shrink to an *icon* on the bottom of the screen. Place the mouse cursor over the Maximize button and press the left mouse button; this will cause the window to expand to the largest size possible. Place the mouse cursor on the resize handles and press the left mouse button; this allows you to move the sides of the window and create a new size for the window. Place the mouse cursor on the Window Menu and press the left button; this will summon a menu that is attached to every window.

Reality Check: Window Managers

The window manager controls all aspects of your computing when you're working with a graphical interface. A window manager may not allow you to resize a window in the manner you desire, nor may a window manager even place a name on the title bar. In other words, the window manager is a despot that you cannot overrule.

This Chapter in Review

▲ In order to put a friendlier face on your computing experience, UNIX allows the use of a graphical interface to make the operating system easier to use.

▲ The most popular graphical interface in the UNIX world is the X Window System, as well as two variants based on it: OSF/Motif and OpenWindows.

▲ On most system featuring a graphical interface, the interface is set up to start automatically after you login the system.

▲ X assumes you have a mouse. However, what the mouse does depends on the X implementation.

▼

▲　**Xterm**, a terminal emulator that brings up a UNIX prompt, is probably the most popular X Window application. An **xterm** window allows you to issue your UNIX command lines directly from a window.

▲　X is sometimes a fragile creature. Don't be surprised to see a number of error messages when you attempt to perform routine tasks. If these error messages persist, see your system administrator.

▲　Even though there can be several windows on the screen, only one can accept your direct input. This is known as the window with focus.

▲　**Mwm** places a title bar and a number of decorations around a window. The title bar gives you the name of the application and allows you to move the window, while the decorations allow you to manipulate the window in several ways.

▲　Window managers have the final say on anything. It is impossible to overrule them. If you have an argument with a window manager, you will always lose.

▪ CHAPTER NINE ▪
Multitasking

A feature that differentiates the UNIX operating system from other operating systems is its ability to do more than one thing at once, called *multitasking*. You don't need to explicitly call on multitasking abilities when performing your daily work, but there are some instances where you'll want to use these abilities. Topics in this chapter include:

- ▲ The principles behind multitasking.
- ▲ Running commands in the background.
- ▲ Listing processes with the **ps** command.
- ▲ Stopping processes with the **ps** command.
- ▲ Commands that explicitly make use of multitasking.
- ▲ Using the **nice** command to run commands nicely.
- ▲ Using the **at** command to run commands at a given time.
- ▲ Using the **batch** command to run a series of commands in the background.
- ▲ Telling commands to run after you've logged off, through the **nohup** command.

▼

Multitasking: Doing More Than One Thing At Once

A prime reason UNIX has become such a popular operating system is its ability to do more than one thing at once.

This is not a capability to be taken lightly in the computer world. If you've used computers at all, you've probably run across situations where you've wanted to do more than one thing at once, but was limited by the operating system from doing so. With UNIX, you can be devoting your attention to one task—in the parlance, running the command in the *foreground*—while the system follows through with another command silently—in the parlance, running the other command in the *background*. Put together, this capability is called multitasking, and it's exactly what the name says: running more than one task at once.

This is technical

Computer geeks love to argue about exactly what constitutes multitasking (as if anyone really cares about the difference between preemptive multitasking and time-slicing). Don't be sucked into arguments about multitasking. Just rest assured that UNIX features the most superior, purest form of multitasking.

From your viewpoint, multitasking, which is managed by the shell, is quite simple. When you enter a command in the system and tell the shell that you want to run the command in the background, the shell throws up another prompt, telling you that it's ready for another command while the background command chugs forth. In fact, depending on your system, the command can keep running even after you log off the system.

Running Commands in the Background

Running a command in the background is a simple matter: Add an ampersand (&) to the end of the command line. The shell then assigns a process ID, or PID, to the command and throws up a prompt, indicating that it's open for further commands:

▼

▼

```
$ sort file1 file2 > file.sort &
[1] 2445
$
```

In this case, you're sorting two files in the background. Sorting files—especially large files—can take quite a bit of time, so it's a good idea to run the **sort** command in the background.

Don't worry about the exact process ID. There's really no reason why you'll need to remember the number. If there is an occasion to reference the process ID, there are UNIX tools (which you'll cover shortly) that can retrieve the ID.

The shell will inform you when the background command is completed.

Listing Processes

There's no limit to how many commands you can run in the background. There are also cases when you're running commands in the background when you don't realize it: For instance, if you're running the X Window System and a graphical interface, you're already running commands in the background automatically.

Still, there may be occasion when you want to check on the background command. You may begin a large task and then decide to cancel it, for instance—such as the sort command, after you decide that the resulting file isn't worth the fuss. In this instance, you'll use the **ps** command to find the PID:

```
$ ps
PID TTY   TIME COMD
681 pts001  0:03 ps
679 pts001  1:21 sh
$
```

237
▼

There are four parts to this listing:

▲ The process ID (PID), which is the unique number assigned to the background command by the UNIX system.

▲ The terminal (TTY) that originated the command.

▲ The amount of time (TIME) the process has been running.

▲ The command name (COMD).

You'll notice that the **ps** command also listed itself, in a case of the Heisenberg uncertainty principle applied to the UNIX system. In addition, the command will also list the shell as a current process. These listings will be present every time you run the **ps** command.

The output from the **ps** command on a larger UNIX system can be voluminous. You may want to send the results of this command to a file, using the wonderful redirection commands you've already covered in this book.

After you've run the **ps** command, you can use the information to kill the process. The UNIX command to do so, eerily enough, is **kill**. Using the results of the above **ps** command as a reference, you can kill the **sort** command with the following command line:

```
$ kill 21087
```

The Command Reference for the **ps** command is listed in Table 9.1.

TABLE 9.1 COMMAND REFERENCE FOR THE PS COMMAND

ps *options*

PURPOSE

The **ps** command lists the status of all current processes.

In BSD UNIX, the options are slightly different; for instance, use **ps-aux** instead of **ps-ef**. In these cases, check your system documentation.

OPTIONS

-a   Displays all processes.

-d   Displays all processes, except group leaders.

-e	Displays information on every process.
-f	Displays full information about processes, including **UID, PID, PPID, C, STIME, TTY, TIME,** and **COMMAND.**
-l	Displays a long listing, which includes such information as priorities set with the **nice** command—and much, much more. (Don't use this option unless you are ready for a *very* long listing.)

Commands That Use Multitasking

With multitasking, you can set up commands to run in the background and essentially forget about them until they are through running. A few UNIX commands take advantage of this capability.

The Nice Command

Every UNIX should be a nice user. In this context, however, *nice* refers to a specific situation.

When you use the **nice** command, you're telling the system to run the command at the system's leisure, not devoting a ton of system resources to the command. This command is quite useful when you're anticipating a long lunch and you want to sort that huge file so it's ready when you return.

A typical **nice** command line would look something like this:

```
$ nice option command argument(s)
```

where *command* is the name of the command you want to run nicely, *option* refers to the only option available with this command (don't worry—for the most part, you won't need to use this option), and *argument(s)* refers to the argument(s) you want the command to use as input. In short: You'd use your normal command line in conjunction with the **nice** command—the only difference is that you stick **nice** at the beginning of the command line.

▼

The Command Reference for the **nice** command is listed in Table 9.2.

TABLE 9.2 THE COMMAND REFERENCE FOR THE NICE COMMAND

> *nice option command argument(s)*
>
> **PURPOSE**
>
> The **nice** command runs a command nicely by giving it a very low priority.
>
> **OPTION**
>
> *-n*   Allows you to set a priority level for the command. The default is 10.

The At Command

The **at** command pretty much does exactly what the name implies: It runs a command line *at* a specified time.

In this instance, the UNIX command is keeping track of the **at** command as a current process, and when the specified time arrives, the **at** command then runs the command line.

There really aren't many circumstances where you'll need to use the **at** command. It's a handy thing to save computational-heavy commands for the middle of the night, when there's no one else using the system and no one to irritate when you're tying up the laser printer with a 2,000-page document. However, system administrators will find the command to be of greater use.

You'll use the **at** command on its own command line in conjunction with time you want a command line to run. For instance, the following command line would run a command at 11 p.m.:

```
$ at 11pm
```

▼

After you press the **Return** or **Enter** key, the cursor will appear on the following line *without* a prompt. It's at this point that you'll enter the command line you want to run at 11 p.m. When you're through with the command line, press **Ctrl-D** to tell the **at** command that you're through entering the command line, *not* the **Enter** key.

You can use the **at** command to run several command lines at a specified time. In this case, press **Enter** at the end of each command line and then press **Ctrl-D** when you're finished entering command lines.

When you're through entering command lines, the **at** command will display a job-ID, confirming that the job will run at a certain time. To see a list of pending jobs generated with the **at** command, use the following command line:

```
$ at -1
```

To remove a job scheduled with the **at** command, you'll need to job-ID (as listed with the *-1* option) and then use the *-r* option to **at**:

```
$ at -r job-ID
```

where *job-ID* refers to the ID number returned by the *-1* option.

The **at** command is not available to every user on every system. In many cases, usage of this command is limited to system administrators. In these situations, you'll get the following error message when you try and use the **at** command:

```
at: you are not authorized to run at. Sorry.
```

The Command Reference for the **at** command is listed in Table 9.3. As you can tell, the **at** command can sometimes be very involved.

TABLE 9.3 THE COMMAND REFERENCE FOR THE AT COMMAND

at *option1 time [date] increment*
at *option2 [job-id]*

TABLE 9.3 CONTINUED

PURPOSE

The **at** command performs specified commands at given times and dates, as long as the commands require no additional input from you.

There are two sets of options available with the **at** commands. One set, *option1*, relates to setting the targeted time and date. The second set, *option2*, allows changes to jobs already scheduled.

After you enter the **at** command, you type in the commands to execute at that time. You type in these commands at the keyboard. When you're finished, press **Ctrl-D**.

At the given time, **at** runs your commands. Any output from the commands is sent to you via electronic mail.

OPTIONS RELATING TO SCHEDULING

-f *filename*	Executes the commands listed in *filename*, rather than the commands input from the keyboard. (Not available on all systems.)
-m	Notifies the user when the job is completed on the screen, instead of via electronic mail.

TIME OPTIONS

time	The time when the commands should run. Unless you specify otherwise (with am or pm as a suffix), the system assumes military time.
midnight **noon** **now**	These options are used in lieu of a specific time. If you use **now** as an option, you must specify an increment (see the following).

DATE OPTIONS

date	Format is usually specified as *month, day, year,* with year optional.
day	The specific day when the command should run, with the name either spelled out (*Sunday*) or referred to by the first three letters (Sun).

| today | These options are used in lieu of a specific date. |
| tomorrow | |

OPTIONS RELATING TO ALREADY-SCHEDULED JOBS

| -l | List current job. |
| -r | Remove specified job. |

INCREMENT OPTIONS

| *increment* | A numerical value relative to the current time and date. The increment must contain a reference to **minute, hour, day, week, month**, or **year**. In the case of *at now + 2 week*s), the job would be performed two weeks from now. |

The Batch Command

Similar to the **at** command is the **batch** command.

Instead of running through a series of command lines *at* a specified time, the **batch** command runs through a series of command lines immediately. These command lines are run in the background, which means the system doesn't put a particularly high priority on them. Again, this command is useful when you're performing some basic chores and aren't in a hurry to complete them.

Using the **batch** command is a matter of the following command line:

```
$ batch
```

As with the **at** command, the cursor appears on the following line *sans* prompt, letting you know that the **batch** command is waiting for input. Enter your command lines, ending each with the **Return** key (or the **Enter** key, depending on your system). When you're through entering command lines, type **Ctrl-D**.

The **batch** command will then run the commands in the order they were entered in the system. You'll receive no feedback from the system as commands are executed; instead, you'll be sent a mail message telling you that the command is complete (or, if the command requires some feedback sent to you, you'll receive this feedback also via mail). In addition, the **batch** command makes sure that each command line is finished, even if the system goes down.

The **batch** command is summarized in Table 9.4.

TABLE 9.4 COMMAND REFERENCE FOR THE BATCH COMMAND

> **batch**
>
> **PURPOSE**
>
> The **batch** command runs a series of commands one command at a time in the background.
>
> **OPTIONS**
>
> *None.*

The Nohup Command

If you begin a task and aren't sure if it will be completed before you hit Happy Hour, you may want to use it in conjunction with the **nohup** command.

The **nohup** (which stands for *no* hang*up*) command tells the command line to continue running even after you log off the system. A typical **nohup** command line looks like the following:

```
$ nohup command arguments filename(s) &
```

where *command* is the name of the command you want to run, *arguments* refers to the arguments for the *command* (not for **nohup**) and the *filename*(s) used as input for the command. In addition, you'll probably want to run the **nohup** command in the background.

There's really not too much more to the **nohup** command, as you'll see from Table 9.5.

TABLE 9.5 COMMAND REFERENCE FOR THE NOHUP COMMAND

nohup *command arguments* &

Purpose
The **nohup** keeps a command running even if you log off the system.

OPTIONS
None.

This Chapter in Review

▲ The UNIX operating system allows you to run more than one command at a time.

▲ This ability is called multitasking. You don't need to know about the specifics of multitasking to make use of this ability.

▲ Commands can be run in the background, which means that they don't have the full attention of the system. To tell a command to run in the background, attach an ampersand (&) to the end of the command line.

▲ You can run any number of commands in the background. (Depending on your system configuration, you may be running several commands without knowing it.)

▲ To check on the status of all commands running on the system, use the **ps** command. It returns a list of all processes, including their filenames, an ID number, and how long they have been running.

▲ With this ID number, you can stop a process. The command for this, appropriately enough, is **kill**.

▲ The **nice** command tells the system to run a command *nicely*—that is, not with the full devotion of the system, but not exactly in background, either.

▲ The **at** command allows you to run a command line, or series of command lines, at a specific time, even if you're not logged on the system.

▲ The **batch** command allows you enter a series of command lines, which are then run in background and in sequence.

▲ The **nohup** command tells a command line to continue running, even after you log off the system.

▪ CHAPTER TEN ▪
System Administration 101

Not every UNIX system has the luxury of a full-time system administrator. In these circumstances, users will need to perform some of the basic system-administration tasks, such as starting the system, making backups of files, and shutting down the system on occasion. This chapter covers the following topics:

▲ Situations where you must act as system administrator.

▲ Logging in the system as the root user.

▲ Setting the system's date and time with the **date** command.

▲ UNIX system states and how to change them.

▲ Backing up your work with the **tar** command.

▲ Extracting archived files with the **tar** command.

▲ Shutting down the system with the **shutdown** command.

▲ Making sure the system is ready to be shut down with the **sync** command.

▲ Alternatives to the **shutdown** command.

System Administration for the Unwilling

Throughout this text, you've been advised to ask your system administrator whenever there's any doubt regarding your next step or when there are system-specific issues to be addressed—in short, when you need an answer to any question.

If you're a corporate user, there's a pretty good chance that you have a system administrator for your system, especially if your UNIX system is on the larger side. However, the reality of the corporate computing world—as well as the reality of the modern business world—is that not every UNIX installation has a system administrator available 24 hours a day. And the reality is that for many smaller UNIX installations (10 users or fewer) there's no such thing as an on-site system administrator, but rather $100-per-hour consultants who monitor the system in order to avoid catastrophes. In these cases, it's not cost-effective to bring in the consultant for every little chore.

And don't forget the single-user UNIX systems. While these don't comprise a large portion of the UNIX computing world, there are nevertheless situations where a person has opted for a single-user UNIX system. Generally speaking, these people are using UNIX because of specialized software available only for the UNIX operating system.

In all of these situations, users must tackle some rudimentary system-administration tasks on your own. The tasks presented in this chapter are among the most rudimentary system-administration tasks available. For the most part, they involve readily accessible UNIX commands. If you're not comfortable with UNIX usage by now, don't attempt to use these commands or carry out these procedures.

The Root User

To get at some of these commands, however, you'll need to login as the *root user* or the *superuser*. This account is indeed the "super" account; with it, you have the ability to perform many actions not available to

▼

the normal garden-variety account you've been using. For example, the root user can override the file permissions set up by normal users—switching files that were read-only for all users to executable for all users. The root user can set up accounts and change passwords. There's no file, including files containing mail and passwords, that can't be accessed by the root user. In short, the root user controls all aspects of UNIX system usage and configuration.

However, logging in as the root user may be either a simple or difficult matter. If you are working on a newly installed system, you may be able to login directly as root, as in the following:

```
Login: root
Password:
#
```

When the system asks you for the password, press the **Enter** key. If this doesn't work, try using **root** both as the password and the logname. This exchange would take place wherever there's a login prompt. A newly configured UNIX system probably doesn't have a password, or has a password of **root**.

The previous login procedure was successful. How can we tell? Because there's a # prompt—and only root users are entitled to that prompt.

If your system was set up by a consultant with continuing responsibilities for the system, you'll have to get root user's password from this person. You'll also have to tell the consultant *why* you need this password and level of access, since the consultant controls the usage of this password and may be justifiably wary of an inexperienced user wanting access to the entire system. (The consultant will also be protecting his turf. The less you know about UNIX, the more billable hours for him.)

Setting the Date and Time

One of the more common reasons for a beginner to be messing around as system administrator is to set the date and time. A new system doesn't know what time it is; rather, the system begins tracking time only after

▼

it has been told the current date and time. (Some PC-based UNIX systems, such as UnixWare, use the system clock found on every PC to determine the date and time.)

To set the current date and time, you'll use the **date** command. However, in this situation the **date** command works differently than it does when you use it as an ordinary user. When used by the root user, it sets the date and time for the system. When used by an ordinary user, it merely *returns* the current date and time.

You must be exact with this command, or else you'll enter an incorrect date and time. The command line is:

```
# date mmddttttyy
```

where *mm* refers to month (01 for January, 02 for February, through 12 for December), *dd* refers to day (01 for the first day of the month, 10 for the tenth day, and so on), *tttt* refers to time (using 24-hour military notation), and *yy* refers to year.

The following command line sets the date for January 1, 1994, for 1:30 a.m.:

```
# date 0101013094
Sun Jan 1 1:30:00 CDT 1994
```

You must remember to include the zeroes when referring to single-numeral instances like 1, 2, and so on; in these cases, you're referring to 01, 02, and so on through 09.

You'll notice the presence of *CDT* in the previous date. CDT stands for Central Daylight Time, and it refers to the time zone that the system is set up to use. Time zones are actually a function of an environment variable (which were covered in Chapter 4) and not of the **date** command.

▼

States of Being and Nothingness

When you start mucking around as a system administrator, there are many side issues that you had no idea even existed. However, there's one important issue that you'll need to worry about: *states*.

A UNIX system runs in five different states. As a user, you didn't need to worry about states, as this was something set up by the system administrator. In this instance, the system was set up in *multiple-user* state, which meant that other users could login the system and access the local filesystem. Most UNIX systems are set up to start in multiple-user state. (This is not true across the board. Apple's A/UX is set up to start in a single-user state.)

There are several system states, which are listed in Table 10.1.

TABLE 10.1 UNIX SYSTEM STATES

STATE	EFFECT
0	*Shutdown*. The system is either off or ready to be powered down.
1	*Administrative*. The full system is available to the root user, but other users cannot login.
2	*Multiple user*. Other users can login the system.
3	*RFS*. Remote filesystems can be mounted, which means that any user has access to these remote systems.
S	*Single-user*. Only a single user can login the system and use the filesystem.

You'll want to make sure and stay in multiple-user state when you are logged in as the root user. Some systems default to administrative status when the root user is logged in (though, admittedly, this is a rare occurrence). You'll know this, as you'll see a line like the following appear on your screen:

```
init 1
```

To change to multiple-user state, use the following command line:

```
# init 2
```

Backing Up Your Work Regularly

If you're working on a standalone system, there's one task you should perform regularly: backing up your files. Nothing is guaranteed in this world, and should there be a disaster of any sort—a power outage, the accidental erasing of an important file—you will need to summon an older version of your work, unless you want to start a project over from scratch.

In many ways, backing up important data is the most important task a system administrator performs. What should you back up? There are three kinds of files stored on your UNIX system: Program files, configuration files, and data files. Program files rarely change and can be reinstalled from the original tape, CD, or floppy disks (though it will occupy a good amount of your time to do so). Configuration files, on the other hand, are a little more important. These are files, like your **.profile** file, that you have adapted for your specific needs. Unless you have a perfect memory, you probably can't re-create them from scratch. Data files are the most important files and should be backed up most often. These files are unique, and if you're like the average business or user, these files comprise the central core of your business. If you lose these files, you've lost the information contained within, as well as the time it took to create them.

The UNIX operating system—or the most recent versions, anyway—features a powerful command for backing up your data: **tar**, which stands for *tape archiver*. You can use **tar** to back up data to any device on your UNIX system—tape drive or floppy disk, for instance. Check your system documentation, as explained in the appendix, or check with your system administrator if you have one. The easiest way to check for this information is with the following command line:

```
# man tar
```

This will display the online-manual page for the **tar** command. The **man** command is explained in the Appendix.

▼

To use **tar** to back up all the files in the current directory, use the following command line:

```
# tar -cvf archivefile .
```

This command does several things. The options do the following:

▲ The *-c* option creates the archive.

▲ The *-v* option tells **tar** to be verbose—in other words, to let you know what's happening and report on the progress.

▲ The *-f* option lists the filename of the archive, in this case **archivefile** (a purely arbitrary choice—you can use whatever filename you'd like).

▲ ., which tells **tar** to backup all of the files in the current directory.

The usage for the **tar** command differs slightly from the rest of the UNIX command set. Options have two parts: A *function* option (each command must contain of these), followed by other options. Table 10.2, the Command Reference for the **tar** command, lists both function options and general options. In addition, the hyphen (-) is not needed before options, although it generally is included.

You can use wildcards with the **tar** command. For instance, to back up all files ending with *txt* in the current directory, you'd use the following command line:

```
# tar -cvf archivefile *txt
```

To back up your files to tape or floppy, you'll need to list the device name of the tape or floppy in place of the filename used here. On most UNIX systems, the tape drive is known as **/dev/tape** (assuming, of course, there is a tape drive). The name of the floppy drive will different from system to system, although most non-PC-based UNIX systems don't have a floppy. (Again, this is not true across the board. Sun SPARCstations, for instance, feature a floppy drive, and it is known as **/pcfs**.)

The following command line backs up all files in the current directory to a tape drive:

```
# tar -cvf /dev/tape .
```

If you want to restore files from the archive, use the following command line:

```
# tar -xvf /dev/tape
```

if you had indeed archived to a tape drive. In this case, you've used the *-x* option, which tells **tar** to extract.

The exact steps you'll use for backing up your data depend on your system configuration. The **tar** command, and to where it backs up data, varies. The examples presented here are generic in their usage.

This is technical

Before you use the **tar** command, make sure that there is a tape in the tape drive. Also, make sure that the tape has stopped moving before you use the command. You can hear the tape whirring in the drive, and some drives need to find a specific place on the tape before they can be accessed by the system.

There are other options associated with **tar**, which are listed in Table 10.2, the **tar** Command Reference.

TABLE 10.2 COMMAND REFERENCE FOR THE TAR COMMAND

tar *options file(s)*

PURPOSE

The **tar** command archives files to **tar** files. Specified files can either replace existing files or be appended to existing files. In addition, **tar** is also used to extract archived files from tape.

FUNCTION OPTIONS

c   Creates a new **tar** archive.

r   Appends *file(s)* to the end of the archive.

t   Prints out a table of contents.

u	Updates an archive by appending *files*, if they are not on the tape or if they have been modified.
x	Extracts files from the **tar** archive.**OPTIONS**
f*dev*	Writes archive to *dev*; the default is **/dev/mt0** on many systems.
o	Changes ownership of extracted files to the current user. This is very useful if the archive was made by another user.
v	Verbose mode: prints out status information.
w	Waits for confirmation.

Shutting Down the System

Most UNIX systems are never turned off, especially larger multi-user systems. Usually, there's really no reason to turn off the system, as it takes a long time to actually get the system up and running—and the more users, the longer the system takes to come up.

However, there are many circumstances where you'll want to shutdown your system, especially if you meet the criteria listed at the beginning of this chapter. If your system supports only one or two users, you'll want to shutdown your system every weekend or even every evening. If you add a peripheral to your UNIX system, you'll need to shutdown the system when you do so. And don't forget to shutdown your UNIX system in hot weather; if your office temperature rises above 85 degrees, it's generally a good idea to shutdown the system.

In the section "States of Being and Nothingness," there was a reference to a system state of 0, which is when the system shuts down. Like the other system states listed in that section, you could use the **init** command to actually shutdown the system.

▼

However, this generally isn't a good idea. Instead, you'll want to use the command **shutdown** to shutdown the system. The **shutdown** switches the system to the shutdown state and alerts all users that the system is going to shut down.

It's also a good idea to use the **sync** command before using the **shutdown** command, especially if you're using an older UNIX system. The **sync** command ensures that the data stored in your system's RAM has been saved to disk. (In theory, the **shutdown** command does this. However, you really should use the **sync** command anyway—don't leave things to chance.)

Using **sync** and **shutdown** together would yield a few command lines like the following:

```
# sync
# shutdown
```

Using the **shutdown** command is usually a little more involved than presented here. After you enter **shutdown** on a command line, the system will ask you a few questions:

▲ If you want to send a message to all users before shutting down.
▲ How long to wait before shutting down the system.
▲ If you really want to shut down the system.

Of course, your answers will depend on your configuration. If you're working on a single-user UNIX system, there's no reason to wait, there's no reason to send a message to yourself—and yes, darn it, of *course* you want to shutdown the system. In this case, you'll want to enter *0* as the amount of time to wait before shutting down the system, as the default is 60 seconds.

Newer versions of UNIX support options to the **shutdown** command, which you'll find quite useful:

```
# shutdown -g0 -y
```

These two options do the following:

▲ The *-g* option specifies the amount of time the system will wait before shutting down, in seconds; in this case, *0* refers to a wait of 0 seconds.

▲ The *-y* option confirms that you really want to shutdown.

After the **shutdown** command runs its course, you'll see the following message:

▼

```
Safe to Power Off
```
- or -
```
Press Any Key to Reboot
```
- or -
```
The system is shutdown.
Press Ctrl-Alt-Del to reboot.
```

 Though these commands are explained under a description of system-administration commands, they can be used on any UNIX system—depending on the system, of course. If you're working on a larger system, don't use the **sync** and **shutdown** commands, and *especially* don't use them just to see if you can.

Alternatives to the Shutdown Command

Some implementations of UNIX, particularly PC-based UNIX systems, contain easier-to-use alternatives to the **shutdown** command. For instance, SCO UNIX features a program called **sysadmsh** that performs the **shutdown** command and much more. **Sysadmsh**, which is really a shell, features menus as a way to perform system-administration tasks. (It's also known on some systems as **sysadm**.)

Novell UnixWare features a graphical interface. One of the icons is **Shutdown**, which saves your current system configuration and then shuts down the system.

This Chapter in Review

▲ Not every UNIX installation has the luxury of a system administrator. In these instances, you'll need to perform some basic system-administration tasks.

▲ To perform these tasks, you'll need to login the system as the root user. The root users has many powers that go well beyond the capabilities of mere mortal users.

▼

▲ One of the most common system-administration tasks involves setting the system's date and time. This is done with the **date** command, which works differently for the root user than it does with mere mortal users.

▲ When working as the root user, you may need to know what state the system is in. A UNIX system can be in five states, ranging from *0* (which is, for all intents and purposes, death) to *S*, which means that only a single user can login the system. Shutting down the system means changing the system state to *0*.

▲ The most important chore of a system administration is regularly backing up important files. These files may contain a key database or other essential data files. To back up these important files, use the **tar** command, which saves these files to a tape archive.

▲ Though most UNIX systems are left running 24 hours a day, there may be instances where you'll want to shut down the system—a long weekend, the installation of a new peripheral, and so forth.

▲ To shutdown the system, first use the **sync** command to make sure that important data in RAM are saved to disk. Then use the **shutdown** command to actually shutdown the system.

■ APPENDIX ■
For More Information

This book is only the beginning of the journey, should you desire to advance your working knowledge of UNIX. This appendix presents further sources of information.

Printed Documentation

If the documentation that came with computer systems was any good, there would be no reason for this book. Have you browsed through the documentation that came with your UNIX system? Ouch.

This documentation serves its purpose: It provides valuable information for the system administrator. The purpose of this documentation is not to provide illumination for the end user. While some system-specific information can be found only in the documentation, the vast amount of it is technical information geared toward the advanced user.

Approach the documentation with a grain of salt: Don't feel inadequate if you don't understand it fully.

Online Manual Pages and the Man Command

One of the neater UNIX commands is **man**, which displays information about UNIX commands.

There's not a lot to the **man** command—essentially, it displays an online manual page about specific UNIX commands. It will not display information about practices and procedures, nor will it display information about specific UNIX topics, like multitasking or processes. Still, it's quite useful for displaying a lot of information about specific commands.

Unfortunately, the **man** command is not fully implemented on some UNIX system, and not at all on other UNIX systems. If you have it, great; if not, lobby your system administrator.

For more information on the man command itself (and assuming you have access to it, of course), use the following command line:

```
$ man man
```

The Command Reference for the **man** command is displayed in Table A.1.

TABLE A.1 COMMAND REFERENCE FOR THE MAN COMMAND

> **man** *command*
>
> **PURPOSE**
> The **man** command displays the online manual page for a command.
>
> **OPTIONS**
> *None.*

▼

Books

As you can tell by a visit to your local bookstore, there are a ton of titles devoted to the UNIX operating system. However, when you start looking at the titles and the tables of contents, you realize that most of them are meant for advanced users and/or system administrators. By contrast, the book in your hands is one of the few books devoted to anyone other than advanced users and/or system administrators, and perhaps the only one devoted only to the UNIX neophyte.

At this point in your UNIX education, though, you may be ready to move on to more advanced tomes. Here are some titles that should aid you in your higher education.

General Titles

Teach Yourself UNIX. Kevin Reichard and Eric F. Johnson, New York: MIS:Press, 1992. This introduction to the UNIX operating system is meant for a more advanced computer user, but still has enough details for the learning beginner. Most of the commands listed in this work are more fully explained in *Teach Yourself UNIX*, while the underlying concepts of UNIX are explained in depth.

UNIX in Plain English. Kevin Reichard and Eric F. Johnson, New York: MIS:Press, 1994. This reference works focuses on in-depth explanations of the important UNIX commands. Definitely the book to be sitting next to your terminal for a quick reference.

X Window System

Using X. Eric F. Johnson and Kevin Reichard, New York: MIS:Press, 1992. This book explains the basics of X Window System usage and configuration. While X Window can be complex, even a beginner is able to handle the very elementary configuration details, as it explains.

▼

Online Sources

As you might expect from a computer system with networking built in, there are many online resources you can tap. The greatest amount of information is carried over the Usenet.

Usenet UNIX Newsgroups

The Usenet is a close cousin to the Internet, which was discussed in Chapter 5. The Usenet, however, contains only newsgroups devoted to discussion of specific topics. Be warned that many of the newsgroups are geared toward various experts, and that some may feel that participation by a UNIX neophyte is not exactly welcome. Asking a general question of a set of UNIX experts is generally met by disdain, rudeness, and techie arrogance. (The exception is the *comp.unix.questions* newsgroup, which is designed specifically for beginners.) If you choose to participate in a specialized topic, you're on your own; the advice from these quarters is to monitor the newsgroups and pick up useful knowledge in that fashion.

In fact, many of the newsgroup feature messages called *FAQs*, or *Frequently Asked Questions*. You'll want to pay special attention to messages with this heading.

General questions are best asked of your system administrator or other UNIX users in your area.

There are many newsgroups on the Usernet devoted to UNIX topics. The list in Table A.2 comes directly from a regular compilation of Usenet newsgroups, who does the public a great service by compiling this list and distributing it to all Usenet users. However, be warned that Table A.2 comprises only a sampling of other UNIX-related newsgroups; other more obscure or specialized newsgroups are omitted.

▼

TABLE A.2 USENET NEWSGROUPS RELATING TO UNIX

NEWSGROUP	PURPOSE
comp.unix.admin	Administering a UNIX-based system.
comp.unix.advocacy	Arguments for and against UNIX.
comp.unix.aix	A discussion of the IBM version of UNIX.
comp.unix.aux	A discussion of the Apple Macintosh version of UNIX.
comp.unix.bsd	A discussion of Berkeley Software Distribution UNIX.
comp.unix.dos-under-unix	A discussion of MS-DOS running under UNIX.
comp.unix.large	A discussion of UNIX on mainframes and in large networks.
comp.unix.misc	Miscellaneous topics.
comp.unix.osf.osf1	A discussion of the Open Software Foundation's OSF/1.
comp.unix.pc-clone.16bit	A discussion of UNIX on 80286 architectures.
comp.unix.pc-clone.32bit	A discussion of UNIX on 80386 and 80486 architectures.
comp.unix.programmer	Q&A for people programming under UNIX.
comp.unix.questions	UNIX neophytes group.
comp.unix.shell	Using and programming UNIX shells.
comp.unix.sys5.r4	A discussion of System V Release 4.
comp.unix.ultrix	A discussion of DEC's Ultrix.

▼

TABLE A.2 CONTINUED

comp.unix.unixware	A discussion of Novell's UnixWare products.
comp.unix.user-friendly	A discussion about UNIX user-friendliness.
comp.unix.wizards	For only true UNIX wizards (moderated).

CompuServe

There are hundreds of forums on CompuServe, but an especially friendly forum for UNIX beginners is the UNIX Forum. Topics in this forum include Forum Info/General, New to UNIX, Communications, Networking, Applications, UNIX OS Topics, DOS under UNIX, and GUI and X Window. This forum also contains software libraries.

▪ GLOSSARY ▪

Absolute pathname	The full name of a file, from the root directory through each subdirectory.
Account	Information about your UNIX usage, such as your username and the way your terminal is configured.
Address	The name of a computer on the network or the name of the entire computer system, used in communications and electronic mail.
Anonymous ftp	Logging on a remote system anonymously to retrieve files (that is, logging in a system without having an account already set up on the system); this method involves limited access to the remote system.
Append	Attach characters to the end of an existing file.
Application	A program that performs a specific task, such as a text editor or a database manager.
Archive	A file that can contain one or more files, serving as a backup (usually on tape) to files on a hard drive.
Arguments	Additions to a command that slightly change the result of the command, either by adding options or specifying filenames.

ASCII	American Standard Code for Information Interchange; a standard format used to store basic alphabetic characters and numerals in a way that any computer—running UNIX or another operating system—can read the file.
Background	A state where commands are run without the full attention and resources of the system; when the commands finish running, the user is notified. Background commands are run from a command line that ends with an ampersand (&).
Bourne shell	See *shell*.
C	Programming language that serves as a basis of UNIX; in addition, most UNIX programs are written in C or its successor, C++.
C shell	See *shell*.
Command	A direct instruction to the computer system.
Command line	The combination of a command and any arguments to the command.
Command prompt	A specific character used by a specific shell in conjunction with the cursor to tell you that the system is ready for a command.
Compressed file	A file that has been shrunk so that it can be transferred more quickly from computer to computer.
Current directory	Your current position on the directory tree.
Cursor	A blinking line or square on the monitor that tells you the system is waiting for a command.
Default	A state or value assumed when no other state or value is present.
Device	A physical device attached to the computer system, such as a modem or tape drive.
Directory	The means for storing files or other directories, analogous to a folder in a file cabinet.

Electronic mail	The electronic equivalent of mail: text messages sent over the UNIX network, either from within the system or from outside the system.
Encryption	A way of encoding a file so it cannot be read by other users.
Environment	Information that determines your UNIX usage and system configuration, as stored in your **.profile** file or set during your computing session.
Error message	A message from the computer system informing you that it cannot perform a specific function.
Executable file	A file containing a program.
FAQ (Frequently Asked Questions)	A list of commonly asked questions on a specific topic (and their answers, of course) disseminated via the Internet.
Field	A vertical column of data from a structured data file, with all of the entries of the same type.
File	The mechanism for storing information on a UNIX system: A set of characters (called *bytes*) referenced by its filename.
Filename	The name for a file.
Filesystem	The method used in UNIX to organize files and directories: A root directory contains several subdirectories, and these subdirectories in turn may contain further subdirectories.
Foreground	Commands that have the full attention of the system and do not return control of the system to the user until the command is complete. In UNIX, the default is to run commands in the foreground.
Freeware	Software created by others and then given away to the computing community at large.
Graphical interface	A graphical display on the monitor, with windows, scrollbars, and icons.

▼

Group	A defined set of users.
Hidden files	UNIX system files that are used for standard housekeeping chores; the filenames begin with a period (.) and are not listed with the **ls** command.
Home directory	A directory where your own files are stored, and where you are placed after you login the system.
Hostname	The name of your UNIX system.
Icon	A graphical representation of a program or file.
Inbox	The storage area for electronic mail that has not been read.
Internet	The umbrella name for a group of computer networks that distributes electronic mail and news-groups around the world.
Keyboard	The big thing you type on to provide input to the computer.
Korn shell	See *shell*.
Link	A file that serves as a reference to another file. Many users can use the same files, making it appear as though they each have their own copy of the file.
Login	To announce your presence to the system by entering your username and password.
Login shell	A script, usually contained in **.login**, that contains basic information about your UNIX usage; this script runs every time you login.
Logname	The name the UNIX system uses to keep track of you. Also known as *username*.
Meta key	A specified key used in conjunction with other keys to create additional key combinations. On most keyboards, the **Alt** key is really the **Meta** key.
Monitor	That big ol' thing sitting on your desk that looks like a television on steroids.

▼

Multiprocessing	When more than one task can be performed simultaneously by the operating system. UNIX is a *multiprocessing* operating system.
Multitasking	When more than one task can be performed simultaneously by the operating system. UNIX is a *multitasking* operating system.
Multiuser	When more than one user can be using the same computer system. UNIX is a *multiuser* operating system.
MS-DOS	An operating system used by most PCs.
Networking	Connecting one computer system to another computer system by direct wiring or phone lines.
Online manual page	Documentation for your system stored within files on the system, accessed with the **man** command.
Operating system	A program that controls all actions of the computer hardware. UNIX is an operating system.
Option	Characters that modify the default behavior of a command.
Ordinary file	A file that is, well, ordinary, containing data or programs, with no special characters.
OSF/Motif	Created by the Open Software Foundation, Motif is actually many things—but for you, the most important thing is that it defines a look and feel for the graphical interface. Based on the X Window System.
Owner	The user with the ability to set permissions for a file.
Parent directory	The directory containing a subdirectory.
Password	A unique set of characters that the UNIX system uses to verify your existence when you want to login the system.
Permissions	A security tool used to determine who can access a file.

Pipe	A conduit between two commands, which tells the second command to use the output from the first command as input.
Process	Essentially, a program running on the computer.
Process ID (PID)	Number assigned by the system to a command.
Program	A set of instructions for the computer to carry out.
Prompt	See *command prompt*.
Redirection	Changing the standard input/output; for instance, saving output to a file instead of printing it to the screen.
Relative pathname	A filename in relation to the current directory position.
Root directory	The top-most directory on the directory tree; every directory on a UNIX system is a subdirectory of the root directory. Indicated in all pathnames as a slash (/).
Root user	The user who can do just about anything possible within the UNIX operating system. Also referred to as the *superuser*.
Server	A computer that supplies files and services to other computers.
Shell	Software that acts as a buffer between you and your operating system. There are many different UNIX shells—the Bourne shell, the Korn shell, and the C shell, for example.
Shell script	A text file that serves as a set of instructions for the shell.
Special device files	Files that represent physical parts of the UNIX system, such as tape drives or terminals.
Standard input/output	The UNIX method of processing commands: The standard input comes from the keyboard, and the output goes to the screen.

▼

States	Different levels that a UNIX system runs in, ranging from a single-user state to a multiuser state.
Subdirectory	A directory contained within another directory. In UNIX, every directory is a subdirectory of the root directory.
System administrator	Your hero/heroine—the person responsible for running and maintaining the UNIX system.
Terminal	A monitor, keyboard, perhaps a mouse, and perhaps a CPU.
Text-based interface	An interface where only characters, and not graphics, are used.
Text file	A file containing only ASCII characters and no special characters. A text file can be read by any program.
UNIX	An operating system that supports more than one user and can perform more than one command at a time—and, of course, the greatest operating system in the world.
Username	The name the UNIX system uses to keep track of you. Also known as *logname*.
Variable	A symbol or character that has different meanings based on context and specific usage.
Wildcard	Special characters within a filename that tell the shell to look for all files with similar filenames.
Window manager	A program within the X Window System that controls the look and feel of the interface.
Working directory	See *current directory*.
Workstation	A computer optimized for running UNIX. Sun SPARCstations and IBM RS/6000s are workstations.
X terminal	A terminal that runs only the X Window System and draws most of its computing power from the network.

X Window System   Graphical windowing system used for building graphical interfaces, like Motif.

xterm   Popular X Window System program that provides a command-line interface to the UNIX operating system.

▪ INDEX ▪

▼

▼